THE LIBRARY OF GRAPHIC NOVELISTS™

NEIL GAIMAN

STEVEN P. OLSON

The Rosen Publishing Group, Inc. New York

To Harp, my daytime collaborator

Published in 2005 by The Rosen Publishing Group, Inc.
29 East 21st Street, New York, NY 10010

Library of Congress Cataloging-in-Publication Data

Olson, Steven P.
Neil Gaiman / by Steven P. Olson.— 1st ed.
    p. cm. — (The library of graphic novelists)
Includes bibliographical references and index.
ISBN 1-4042-0285-4 (library binding)
1. Gaiman, Neil. 2. Novelists, English—20th century—Biography.
3. Graphic novels—History and criticism. 4. Graphic novels—
Authorship.
I. Title. II. Series.
PR6057.A319Z825 2005
813'.54—dc22

                                    2004011070

Manufactured in Malaysia

CONTENTS

INTRODUCTION

Neil Gaiman is a lean Brit who, as he admits on his Web site, "has somehow reached his early forties and still tends to need a haircut." He wears black because it goes with everything. To the legion of fans that buy his books and come to his readings, he is always polite. He looks and acts like an ordinary fellow.

What is extraordinary about Gaiman lies hidden behind his shaggy mop of hair and dark eyes. Gaiman once described his brain as a tape recorder that's switched on all the time. All sights, sounds, and words of interest are recorded for use at some future date. This exceptionally acute memory has helped Gaiman become one of the most versatile storytellers today.

Gaiman is a writer, and although he dabbles in drawing, it is through writing that he has added so much to the genre of graphic novels. When Gaiman sits down

Neil Gaiman is one of the most widely read graphic novelists in print. His interest in many different methods of storytelling and his ability to craft a tale that can be read on a variety of levels make him very popular among readers.

at his computer to write, at his fingertips are deep and clear memories from his life and from all of the books, comics, anecdotes, and other stories that he has read or heard. From this massive archive, he pulls the best bits and pieces and mixes them with his very active imagination. The results are masterful stories that blend horror, fantasy, and the classics.

Although he loves to draw from many sources, Gaiman's favorites are myths—those stories that have stood the test of time because they offer explanations for something fundamental or important about the human experience. Myths are not limited to stories about the gods of ancient Greece; every culture generates its own myths. For Gaiman, myths are the collective recorded dreams of a culture—and full of rich material for his stories. As he notes in an interview in *Comic Book Rebels*, "How people see the world, how the world sees people; what stories people create to allow them to cope with and interpret the world. Myths are almost the rules of the game. They tell you rules and truths, even if the truths are not necessarily what they ought to be . . . Myths are my favorite subject."

Never content to simply retell a story, Gaiman blends mythic tales with elements from the vast library of recorded material between his ears. Always one to test the limits of a story and his own ability to tell it, Gaiman found an ideal format in which to conduct his tests, a forum for which the rules were far from set in stone: the graphic novel.

A Brief, Brief History of the Graphic Novel

In 1978, renowned artist Will Eisner released a comic called *A Contract with God* that featured the phrase "graphic novel" on a comics cover for the first time. Although the concept of graphic novels had been debated in the comics industry since the 1960s, Eisner claims in an interview for *Time* that the term came to him by accident while pitching the book to a New York editor: "A little voice inside me said, 'Hey, stupid, don't tell him it's a comic or he'll hang up on you.' So I said, 'It's a graphic novel.'"

Eisner's admission contains much of the struggle for comics artists; up until very recently, they just weren't taken seriously. Although comics artists such as Eisner were far from stupid and worked long hours to develop the skills to write, pencil, ink, color, and letter their stories, their work was relegated to the children's section at bookstores. At the time, a heavy set of industry standards prevented artists from creating characters and stories in which good and evil were not clearly defined. In most comics stories, the purely good superhero fought the purely evil villain and triumphed. These stories were often simple constructions in a fantastic yet dull America. Kids bought piles of these comics, so publishers saw no reason to take chances on new material. As kids grew older, they just drifted away.

In the early 1980s, a wave of British artists crashed the American comics scene. Led by rebels such as Alan Moore and Grant Morrison, these writers and artists sought to push superhero comics in new directions. As children, they had eagerly consumed American comics, and they yearned to tell stories that they and their adult friends would enjoy. While comics like Moore's *Marvelman* were rooted in superhero characters and twenty-four-page formats, the content of the stories sought to push the boundaries of what was acceptable in comics form. Much to the delight of the publishers, these comics began to sell, often to adults on whom comics publishers had long ago given up.

After the first wave of new talent landed, Neil Gaiman was right behind them. A reader of comics as a boy, Gaiman was drawn back to them when he read Moore's *Swamp Thing* comic in a London train station in 1984. A few months later, Moore himself taught Gaiman how to script a comic, and a new comics writer was born.

In the more than twenty-five years since Eisner coined the term, the graphic novel medium has expanded in form and grown in sales. In bookstores, it now covers an extremely broad range of materials, from bound collections of *Superman* comics to Japanese Manga books to works of literature and art by creators such as Neil Gaiman. Nevertheless, few artists like the term or the fact that their works are all lumped together on the same shelf. Artists such as Eisner, Moore, and Gaiman know that what they produce has literary and artistic importance. However, their medium has no suitable name.

Are they graphics? Are they novels? Where does a loose-leaf comic end and a graphic novel begin? Is the category determined by a page count or perhaps by the type of story? The uncertainty in comics today suggests that there is much territory in the form left to explore.

There is magic unique to graphic novels. In leaping from panel to panel on a comics page, Scott McCloud says in his masterful book, *Understanding Comics*, "The comics creator asks us to join in a silent dance of the seen and the unseen. The visible and the invisible. This dance is unique to comics. No other art form gives so much to its audience while asking so much from them as well. This is why I think it's a mistake to see comics as a mere hybrid of the graphics arts and prose fiction. What happens between these panels is a kind of magic only comics can create."

A Note About Gaiman's Work

Neil Gaiman's material is not for everyone. He presents adult subjects in a frank manner. The visuals are often disturbing. Young children may be alarmed at the imagery and confused by the stories.

However, Gaiman's unique vision has reopened the door of comics to more mature readers who have otherwise dismissed them as being just for kids. His stories draw upon myths and ideas from the dawn of written history. Their currents run deep.

It is impossible to understand on first reading all of the subtleties and references in his stories. Likewise, this book cannot explain the sum total of Neil Gaiman's comics, for there is simply too much material. This book may serve as an introduction to Gaiman's work or as a partial explanation of some of it. Readers are then encouraged to revisit Gaiman's fine stories. For, like all quality literature, they never lose their flavor when consumed again and again.

CHAPTER 1

THE DREAMING

he promise of revolution in comics began on November 10, 1960, in Portchester, on the southern coast of England. Neil Richard Gaiman was born above the grocery store that his parents owned. By the time he and his family left the area five years later, young Neil had already found his way into the world of letters.

A Writer Is Born in Reading

From a very young age, Gaiman's mother inspired him to read and write. Before his fourth birthday, he composed his first poem. In his interview with Hy Bender for *The Sandman Companion*, Gaiman remembers his childhood relationship with books: "I'd always carry books around with me. My parents would frisk me before we went to a family gathering, like a wedding or a bar mitzvah, because they assumed I had a book on me somewhere. And they were right; I'd usually spend the day under a table reading."

As a boy, Gaiman did not discriminate between the plays of Shakespeare and the fantasy stories of C. S. Lewis, James Branch Cabell, and J. R. R. Tolkien. He read anything and everything.

In 1967, a friend of Gaiman's father lent him a boxful of comic books. From that single box of stories grew an enduring romance between Gaiman and the world of comics. At the time, comics featuring superheroes such as Batman, Superman, Wonder Woman, Spider-Man, and the Hulk topped the sales charts. Coming from America, these comics gave young Neil a striking impression of that country across the Atlantic. These comics presented America and the legends of the Norse gods in a similar way—heroic figures completing monumental challenges in a vast and seemingly magical landscape. It is easy to imagine an impressionable boy falling in love with these stories, these dreams of myth and America.

By the time he became a teenager, Gaiman knew that he wanted to write comics for a living. He was sent to the Whitgift School, an all-boys boarding school in South Croydon. Founded in 1596, the school is housed in stately brick buildings on immaculate grounds with beautiful roses and old statues of solemn-faced men. Boys are required to wear coat and tie to class. By all appearances, it is a proper British boarding school for future men of importance.

Even as a young boy, Neil Gaiman loved books, plays, and poems, and showed a prodigious talent for writing. This photograph shows a young Gaiman of age three or four, a time in his life from which he would later draw inspiration for the characters and the situations in *Violent Cases*.

If Gaiman's story of Charles Rowland is any indication, young Neil hated boarding school. In the "Season of Mists" story line of Gaiman's *Sandman* series, young Rowland is left alone at a stately boarding school over the Christmas holiday and is tortured by the ghosts of cruel older boys. Rowland becomes ill, retreats to the attic of the school, and withers and dies. In *The*

Sandman Companion, Gaiman admits, "Charles Rowland is largely me." The difference was that Gaiman's experience was much less dramatic. Unlike Rowland, Gaiman merely graduated.

But attending an old boarding school did have its privileges. In a 1999 interview for the Writers Write Web site, Gaiman fondly recalls the school libraries filled with old books: "I'd sit up there devouring the complete works of Edgar Wallace or G. K. Chesterton. In fact, I remember my first encounter with *Lord of the Rings* was the first two books in battered old hardcovers . . . And when I was about twelve I won the school English prize and they said, 'What would you like as a present? You get a book.' I said, 'Please can I have the *Return of the King,* so that I can find out what happens.'"

At fifteen, Neil met with a guidance counselor at school. When the counselor asked him what he wanted to do for a living, he said, "I want to write American comic books." Instead of directing him to a school of visual design or a college with a fine writing program, the counselor suggested he go into accounting. Hurt and discouraged, Gaiman did not read comics for nine years.

Nevertheless, Gaiman continued to read, notably the writers of 1960s new wave science fiction. In 1964, Michael Moorcock became the editor of *New Worlds,* a science-fiction magazine that published stories about space creatures and swordsmen. Tired of standard science fiction, Moorcock took chances on writers such as J. G. Ballard and Brian Aldiss. For these writers, technology was not necessarily to be worshiped. Technology had plunged the world into the Cold War, a fight to build the most and largest nuclear weapons. Technology had pushed America and Russia into space, where someday the war to end war might be fought. The fiction of Ballard, Samuel R. Delany, and Roger Zelazny questioned the value of technology. In their science-fiction stories and novels, the emphasis was on the fiction, not the science, and on the emotional lives of characters caught in technologically advanced worlds. In his interview for *The Sandman Companion*, Alan Moore recalls the inspiration that he drew from the new wave writers: "Just to see one could write that way, that you could take an old form and create something completely unanticipated with it, was highly inspiring . . . I imagine Neil got a certain amount of rocket fuel from that as well."

Birth of a Writer

Despite the guidance counselor's negative advice, young Neil did not give up his dreams of writing. Shortly after graduation from high school, he began to write stories, which he submitted to various publications. Although some editors returned them with kind notes of encouragement, no one bought any of his stories.

After eighteen months of luckless effort, he decided to take a new approach. As he recalls in *The Sandman Companion*, Gaiman told himself one day, "Either I have no talent—which I do not choose to believe—or

I'm simply not going about this the right way. I'm going to switch to journalism, and in the process I'm going to figure out how the world works—how magazine articles get assigned, how books get published, how television scripts get sold."

When Gaiman decided to become a journalist, he knew little about it and no one in the field. He began calling the editors of his favorite London-based magazines, such as *Time Out*, *City Limits*, the *Observer*, and the *Sunday Times of London Magazine*. Slowly, he began to receive assignments. When he returned stories and interviews that were factually accurate and well-written, these editors began to trust Gaiman's ability to deliver stories.

Hello, Again, Dear Comics

One day in 1984, when Gaiman was waiting for a train at Victoria Station in London, he noticed a rack of comics at a newsstand. Among the comics was *The Saga of the Swamp Thing* number 25. An original series that started and stopped in the 1970s, *Swamp Thing* returned in 1984 with the writing of Alan Moore. What Gaiman read in that train station was a fresh and vigorous approach to comics. Gaiman found himself admiring the quality of the writing, yet he could not accept his own judgments about the work. That guidance counselor's words were still in his head.

About a month later, Gaiman was waiting for another train in Victoria Station when he noticed *Swamp Thing* number 26 on the same newsstand rack.

The Saga of the Swamp Thing number 25 ("The Sleep of Reason") was written by Alan Moore, with artists Stephen Bissette and John Totleben. Published in June 1984, it was edited by DC Comics' Karen Berger, who would prove to be a key player in Neil Gaiman's career. Just as Berger would have Gaiman do, Moore took an old, mostly forgotten character, the Swamp Thing, and retooled it for a modern, savvy audience. The comic book changed Gaiman's life.

Moore had delivered another well-written comic. When Gaiman found *Swamp Thing* number 28 on the rack, he bought it and read it carefully on the train home. As Gaiman recalls in *The Sandman Companion*, "And that was the final straw; what was left of my resistance crumbled. I proceeded to make regular and frequent visits to London's Forbidden Planet shop to buy comics . . . It was like returning to an old flame and discovering that she was still beautiful."

Over the next two years, Gaiman continued to work as a journalist, reviewing films. By his estimate, he reviewed more than 700 films—all of the major releases and some of the minor ones. Most of them, he felt, were a waste of time.

As his professional life continued to expand, so did his personal life. In 1985, he married Mary McGrath, an American, with whom he had two children, Michael and Holly. He was making money, writing for many of his favorite publications, and starting a family. His career as a journalist, however, had ceased to fulfill him. With his free time, he rekindled his love of comics.

In 1985, he cowrote with Kim Newman a book of terrible quotes from science fiction, called *Ghastly Beyond Belief*. Gaiman sent a complimentary copy to Alan Moore. To Gaiman's surprise, Moore, a private person, called a few days later. An important friendship was born.

CHAPTER 2

A NOVEL FORM: COMICS

eil Gaiman found Alan Moore, and then Alan Moore found Neil Gaiman for the rest of us. Several months after Gaiman sent his book to Moore, Gaiman invited Moore to be his guest at the British Fantasy Convention in Birmingham, England, which Gaiman was covering as a journalist. Toward the end of the day, Gaiman asked Moore how to structure a comics script.

The Structure of a Comics Script

Before time and money are invested in developing the art for each panel of a comic, a script allows everyone on the production team to reach a common understanding of the story. Since writing is much easier to edit than artwork, the script format becomes the least expensive way to revise the story.

Ultimately, a comics script has an audience of one: the artist. While each writer has a unique style of scripting, the best ones tailor their style to the artist. As Nat Gertler says in his introduction to *Panel One: Comic Book Scripts by Top Writers*, "The comics writer is not just giving instructions to the artist; he is transferring a vision."

Since he works with a variety of artists, Neil Gaiman's scripts vary in style and format. For example, the formats of the scripts he has sent to artist Dave McKean have changed with each project. In his interview for *Comic Book Rebels*, Gaiman says, "With *Violent Cases*, I wrote it essentially as a short story and handed it over to him and said, 'Okay, now run with it.' With things like 'Hold Me' [*Hellblazer* number 27], or the story I wrote for *Outrageous Stories from the Old Testament*, they were written as formal scripts. You know, 'Page one, panel one.' While *Black Orchid* was scripted like a movie, and *Signal to Noise* was written in some strange bastard form that only myself and McKean could understand a word of. The script would be completely meaningless to anyone else, because they would ignore the fact that we'd been talking on the phone about this for a month and a half, and are, in a way, telepathic."

In the back of the bound collection of "Dream Country," Gaiman includes the script for *Sandman* number 17 that he sent to penciller Kelley Jones. A good exercise is to compare the script to the comic in finished form.

These sketches for "Dream Country" were drawn by Neil Gaiman. As Gaiman sat down to write each *Sandman* installment, he plotted out the panels and actions that he saw in his mind. Then, depending on the artist he would be working with, he would write out a formal script, a short prose story, draw sketches, or even convey his vision to the artist over the telephone.

By the mid-1980s, Alan Moore had established a reputation in the comics industry for including in his scripts every bit of detail and vision in his head. That style of scripting has been passed on to Gaiman. Using Moore's lesson, Gaiman wrote his first comics script. In his interview for *The Sandman Companion*, Gaiman recalled the results. "I sent the script to Alan, and he told me, 'Yeah

Alan Moore has created groundbreaking graphic novels that have taken the genre further than anyone could ever have imagined. Neil Gaiman could not have chosen a better writer from whom to learn. Born on November 18, 1953, in England, Moore got his start writing comic strips before breaking out of the comic formula with *Saga of the Swamp Thing* and *Watchmen*. The quality of Moore's writing was so high that he was able to eliminate traditional comics devices such as thought balloons, captions, and sound effects.

it's all right. The ending's a bit off.' And then he actually used a few lines of my story in *Swamp Thing* number 51, 'Home Free,' which was very encouraging to me."

That encouragement led to another *Swamp Thing* script called "Jack in the Green" and more positive response from Moore. Although he did not know it at the time, Gaiman's life in comics was picking up speed very quickly.

Dave McKean

A few months later, Gaiman had the good fortune to meet the artist Dave McKean. Their talents were complementary; where Gaiman was strong, McKean was still developing—and vice versa. They shared a passion for comics and discovered that they liked each other, too. They've been friends and collaborators for nearly twenty years now.

In 1986, they were collaborating on a comic that was never published when the editor of *Escape* magazine interviewed them about the project. Impressed with their work, he offered them the chance to do a five-page strip for the magazine. After Gaiman and McKean talked it over, they asked the editor if they could develop a forty-page comic book instead. That comic book eventually became *Violent Cases*.

In September of that year, Gaiman attended the UK Comic Art Convention and introduced himself to Karen Berger, an editor from DC Comics in America. Berger had been working with Alan Moore for some time, and she said that Moore had mentioned Gaiman. After that meeting, Gaiman mailed her a copy of his *Swamp Thing* script "Jack in the Green."

Five months later, Berger and Dick Giordano, vice president of DC Comics, returned to England. Gaiman and McKean met them at their hotel and pitched a number of story ideas to them. Out of these ideas, Berger and Giordano wanted them to restart DC's *Black Orchid* series. Gaiman and McKean got to work immediately. By the time Berger and Giordano boarded their plane to return to the United States, they had Gaiman's outline and four paintings by McKean to take with them. Their speed in producing work helped close the deal to develop the new *Black Orchid*.

End of Journalism

By 1986, Gaiman had written many articles for British newspapers and magazines. He had written three books: *Ghastly Beyond Belief*, a short biography of the rock group Duran Duran, and another book that he refuses to acknowledge to this day. Gaiman was becoming disenchanted with journalism.

He quarreled with editors who rewrote his stories. Sometimes the rewrites completely changed the nature of the story. On Gaiman's final day in journalism, he was offered the chance to write a story on the game Dungeons & Dragons. In an interview with Alex Amado, Gaiman recalls his conversation with the newspaper editors, "They said, 'Well, great. Now what we want is an article showing how it drives people mad and makes them use black magic and commit suicide.' There was a vaguely incredulous pause on my side and I said, 'Well, no!' They said, 'Why not?' I said, 'Well, because I'm not working for you anymore,' and I put down the phone. That was really how I quit journalism."

With journalism behind him, Gaiman began to work in earnest on his first love, comics. By the end of 1986, Gaiman had assembled around him the pieces with which to build a career in comics. In artist Dave McKean he had an extremely talented collaborator whose abilities complemented his own. In Alan Moore, he had a mentor to guide him in writing scripts and in the business of publishing comics. And in Karen Berger and DC Comics, he had a relationship with a publisher that would carry him to great heights.

Violent Cases

While they were developing a relationship with DC Comics, Gaiman and McKean were already at work on their project for *Escape* magazine. Because it was their first project together, Gaiman originally penned *Violent Cases* as a prose story. He reviewed it with McKean, who broke down the story into comics pages and panels. Gaiman then rewrote the story in script form and discovered that it was forty pages long. Their first comic had become a graphic novel.

Published in 1987, *Violent Cases* explored the nature of childhood memories through a little boy's trip to the osteopath of legendary gangster Al Capone.

The Story

The unnamed narrator, an adult who looks like Gaiman, recalls the story of an injury he suffered when he was four years old. His father, who accidentally caused the injury, takes him to the osteopath for treatment. The narrator has trouble remembering the details of what follows.

Much of the uncertainty of these memories is reflected in McKean's images of the osteopath. The first image of him is the rough outline of a face blended into a map of central Europe. There is nothing in the face that makes it easy to identify. On the following page are eight panels showing the osteopath, yet none of them provides a clear picture of the man. All of the images are from a child's viewpoint; the reader sees the osteopath's tie, his right eye, and in one image nothing at all. Through the artwork, Gaiman and McKean suggest that the four-year-old boy cannot see the entire picture of the man.

Later in the story, the boy wanders away from a magician's performance at a child's birthday party. At the pub next door to the party, he finds the osteopath drinking alone. In McKean's images, the hair of the osteopath has grown longer and wilder. Then, the narrator interrupts the flow of the story to change our view of the osteopath. He claims that unlike the pictures of him seen so far in the story, the osteopath actually looked younger and refined, "He looks like Humphrey Bogart's partner in *The Maltese Falcon*— although for a while just now I found it hard to remember whether we ever saw Bogart's partner in the

These three panels from *Violent Cases* are good examples of the methods Gaiman and McKean use to depict memory's unreliability. The first panel shows an illustration of the way the narrator incorrectly remembered the osteopath. Like the flash of a realization, the center portion lights up, showing a realistic representation of Humphrey Bogart's partner in the movie *The Maltese Falcon*. The third panel moves the reader to the narrator's revised but hazier memory of the osteopath, clearly showing the influence of this realization.

flesh, or whether he lived and died offscreen. No, we saw him, briefly at the beginning."

Across the bottom of the page, the osteopath appears in the first panel as an older man who looks like Albert Einstein drinking from a glass. The next image shows the actor who played Bogart's partner in *The Maltese Falcon*. In the final panel, the osteopath looks like he was drawn from that picture. In the background of the first and third image is a poster for something called "Wine of Youth." As the osteopath drinks the Wine of Youth, the narrator "drinks" from the memory of this American film and thus changes the reader's view of the osteopath to a much younger man. Here, the adult's memory has been literally colored by his memories of an American movie.

In the pub, the osteopath tells the boy a story from his days in America when he worked for Al Capone. While the osteopath's narration about the events of "Al's big party in twenty nine" are specific and horrible, the accompanying images are highly stylized fragments of the entire scene. Like the boy's first incomplete impressions of the osteopath, the images of Capone murdering a roomful of cronies provide only bits of the whole story. These small pieces are filtered by the windows through which the reader experiences them: an adult is recalling incomplete memories of himself as a four-year-old boy listening to a story told from the osteopath's memory of a distant and mythic landscape. Each of those windows changes the memory in both large and subtle ways.

The impressions of that landscape are further colored by the influence of American culture on the adult's memories. Gaiman spent much of his childhood in England watching American films and reading American comic books, absorbing their images of America. In *Violent Cases*, Gaiman wanted to say something back to those images from his childhood, which he explains in his *Comic Book Rebels* interview. "I've always been fascinated by America. I always figured America was kind of like Oz . . . [The image of] America has always been a 'myth' that I've been fond of, and a myth I like building on and newly creating."

At the end of the story, the boy peeks around a curtain (another filter) in the pub to see the magician from the party standing over the sobbing figure of the osteopath. Against a backdrop of American movie posters, three large, mysterious men enter the pub, surround the osteopath, and escort him outside. The magician then closes the curtain through which the boy has been peeking. The reader's window into the world of the osteopath, incomplete, colored, and even blackened in places, is closed forever; the osteopath is never seen again.

Once again, the reader's perception of an act of violence is incomplete. The images of the three main acts of violence in the story—the boy's injury, the story about Al Capone, and the disappearance of the osteopath—are altered by imperfect memory of the event, other recollections, and uncontrollable imagination. In his first graphic novel, Gaiman suggests that the true facts of events from childhood can never be regained.

Art and Production Notes

A comic doesn't have to have a consistent art style throughout the work, as changes in style of the imagery can be used to better tell the story. In *Violent Cases*, artist Dave McKean demonstrates a strong understanding of that lesson.

Violence in *Violent Cases* is treated with high-contrast images—darker darks and lighter lights, with bright red coloring to suggest blood and rage. The four panels shown above are from the osteopath's story about Al Capone's murder spree. Note the fright and terror elicited from the close-up and skewed angles of the top two panels. The bottom panels effectively represent the horror of the incident by simply using nonhuman representations of violence: the bat as weapon and the blood that is the product of the violence.

The first images of the story are drawn in more realistic detail and come from the known adult world of the narrator. As the images explore the memory of the narrator and the osteopath, they become less realistic. In a panel, the central image is usually drawn in a clear style that's easy to understand, yet the edges of it may fade away. Details are missing, replaced by blank spots, smears, overlapping, or dark highlights. These techniques create an uncertainty about the image that reinforces the uncertainty of memory in the story. The images, after all, are windows into the narrator's memory.

When violence enters the story, it seems to creep into the images in the form of stronger contrast, ink splattered like blood, and more energetic lines. These techniques place more emphasis on the mood of the image. For example, when the osteopath tells the story of Al Capone killing twenty or thirty men on his payroll, McKean adds red highlights to the images to suggest the tension in the room and the bloody violence that is to come.

In other pages, McKean adds a blue tint to the images. These pictures often contain the magician or elements from the adult world, which is magical to the four-year-old child.

Black Orchid (Numbers 1-3)

When he met Karen Berger and Dick Giordano at their hotel in 1987, Gaiman asked Berger if he could create a story based on the DC character Black Orchid. Reportedly, Berger said, "Black Hawk Kid? Who's that?" Thus began Gaiman and McKean's work on *Black Orchid* and their long association with DC Comics. Since *Black Orchid* was the first project Gaiman, McKean, and Berger worked on together, several rounds of revisions to the script were needed. Gaiman and McKean worked on these while completing *Violent Cases*. In the introduction to the 1991 reprint of the three-comic series, writer Mikal Gilmore calls *Black Orchid* "an act of imagination and hope that tries to take a much under-valued form of literature into places where it has never gone before."

The Stories

Originally, Black Orchid was a conventional superhero: a genetic hybrid of an orchid and a human who fights crime. Within the first few pages of Gaiman and McKean's 1988 version, violence forces Black Orchid in a more peaceful direction.

The story begins in conventional territory for comics. As a meeting of crime bosses is ending, a woman is trapped in her seat by titanium cords. Her mask is removed, and the reader meets Black Orchid. Even though Black Orchid breaks free from her titanium binds, she is shot in the head and burned to death. Instead of conquering crime, Black Orchid is a victim of it. In Gaiman's hands, she is then reborn.

Gaiman cuts back and forth between this criminal underworld and the new Black Orchids, who have been growing in a secret laboratory. Famous as the adversary of Superman, Lex Luthor is the criminal mastermind who wants to capture the Black Orchid technology for his own selfish and commercial purposes. Meanwhile a psychopath named Carl Thorne wants to kill the last of the Black Orchids. (The original Black Orchid was his wife. She left him and sent him to prison.) These three separate story lines begin to converge: the two nearly black-and-white stories from the criminal underworld and the lushly colored, sweeter story of the two new Black Orchids struggling for the survival of their hybrid species.

Unlike typical superheroes, these Black Orchids consistently make peaceful choices instead of confronting criminals with violence and aggression. When Carl Thorne kills their creator and attempts to destroy them, the Black Orchids fly away and hide among the trees. Later, when Thorne is thrown in the river to drown, the mother Black Orchid rescues him, saying, "Part of me wants to leave him to the water and the dark. He killed them . . . Part of me knows that saving him can only bring more pain. More hurt. But too many have died today. No more."

When the mother Black Orchid discovers that her daughter, Suzy, is missing, she finds the Swamp Thing in the bayous of Louisiana. Among the closeness of the trees and the safety of the wilderness, the Swamp Thing tells her where she can find Suzy. Taking with her his gift of seeds, she finds Suzy in the hands of Lex Luthor's henchmen. Instead of hurting these kidnappers, the

These three panels from *Black Orchid* are wonderful examples of the lushness and beauty Dave McKean brought to Gaiman's pacifist tale. The three hitmen, so out of place in the dreamy forest, fall under the spell of the Black Orchid and turn the gun over to her.

Black Orchids fly away from them and their gunfire, leaving a single orchid as a calling card.

The Black Orchids attempt to retreat farther and farther from civilization. The men find them in the jungle and fight over them. When Thorne is killed, Luthor's lieutenant, Sterling, orders one of his men to burn down the jungle. The henchman refuses: "Look at her, Sterling. She's perfect. She's beautiful. I—we've killed for you before. It's what we do. But not her. Not here." The perfect beauty of Black Orchid in the jungle has conquered violence. Black Orchid walks up to

Sterling and gently removes the gun from his hand, leaving him with a message for Lex Luthor, "The game is over. I'm tired of it. Tell him if he ever interferes again with me, or my sisters, we will retaliate . . . I didn't mention violence. But if he persists . . . I will find whatever it is that he loves . . . and I will take it away from him. Tell him that."

In *Comic Book Rebels*, Gaiman describes his idea for *Black Orchid*, "I wanted to do a pacifist fable in which acts of violence did occur, but were unpleasant—a fable in which meditation and beauty played a very important part. *Black Orchid* was sort of a look at all the things I didn't like in comics, and then do the kind of comic I would like to be out there."

In *Black Orchid*'s final threat, Gaiman is putting the world of comics on notice that the old, childish game of superheroes, crime, and violence is over, and a new, beautiful day is dawning.

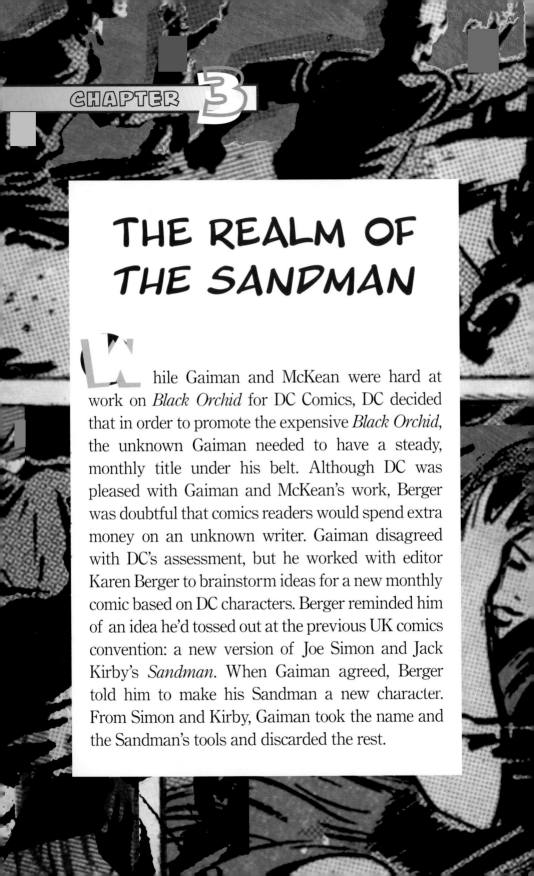

CHAPTER 3

THE REALM OF THE SANDMAN

While Gaiman and McKean were hard at work on *Black Orchid* for DC Comics, DC decided that in order to promote the expensive *Black Orchid*, the unknown Gaiman needed to have a steady, monthly title under his belt. Although DC was pleased with Gaiman and McKean's work, Berger was doubtful that comics readers would spend extra money on an unknown writer. Gaiman disagreed with DC's assessment, but he worked with editor Karen Berger to brainstorm ideas for a new monthly comic based on DC characters. Berger reminded him of an idea he'd tossed out at the previous UK comics convention: a new version of Joe Simon and Jack Kirby's *Sandman*. When Gaiman agreed, Berger told him to make his Sandman a new character. From Simon and Kirby, Gaiman took the name and the Sandman's tools and discarded the rest.

The First Grains of Sand

Shortly after Gaiman received the *Sandman* opportunity, England was hit with its first hurricane in 300 years. Sitting in the dark at home, he thought about a character who would fit into DC's universe yet allow him to write stories that interested him. Whittling the idea to its basics, he came up with the Lord of Dreams.

In dreams can be found all of man's joys, hopes, and fears. This material is pure fuel for a writer's art. For Gaiman, the character of Dream, the master of all dreams, was the perfect vehicle.

Through Dream, who was also called the Sandman and many other names in the series, Gaiman could explore his favorite subject—myths—from cultures all over the world. In an interview with Alex Amado during the *Sandman* years, Gaiman explains, "It's been really fun because you can play with all the mythologies that have gone by, and with the mythologies that are springing up in the twentieth century. So, on the one hand, you have serial killers, who've been assimilated into twentieth century mythology, and on the other hand I can do *Midsummer Night's Dream*, or look at what cats dream about."

As Gaiman suggests, each culture creates its own myths. Whether in ancient Greece or twentieth-century America, a culture's mythic stories often feature heroic characters whose lives are changed by their gods or other forces beyond their control. The gods of the culture define rules with which the heroic characters must live or die. The heroic characters, then, become a test case for the rules of the culture.

Sandman: "Preludes & Nocturnes" (Numbers 1-8)

From the first pages of *Sandman* number 1, it is clear that the comic is no story about superheroes. Trapped and stripped of his mask, amulet, and bag of dream dust, the Sandman lies naked inside a glass dome, the prisoner of a petty human magician. The Sandman does not have clever things to say. He does not even speak. He waits in silence for seventy-two years to escape.

"Preludes & Nocturnes" then details the Sandman's struggle to reacquire the tools of his trade and his power. As the Sandman gets reacquainted with friends, foes, and even Lucifer, the lord of hell himself, the reader gets acquainted with Dream and the unique rules of the Dreaming, his realm.

The Stories

Story by story, Dream gathers his strength and his tools. After his escape, Dream reclaims his dream dust and then ventures to hell, where he outwits a demon to reacquire his helmet. Lucifer vows revenge. Dream's final tool of office, his ruby amulet, is in the possession of Doctor Dee, a madman who escapes Arkham Asylum. Doctor Dee has changed the function of the ruby amulet, and in *Sandman* number 6, he puts those powers on horrible display.

SLEEP OF THE JUST

NEIL GAIMAN
STORY
SAM KIETH &
MIKE
DRINGENBERG
ARTISTS
TODD KLEIN
LETTERS
ROBBIE BUSCH
COLORS
ART YOUNG
ASST. EDITOR
KAREN BERGER
EDITOR

In this panel from *Sandman* number 1, we see Dream, the Sandman, imprisoned and curled up, as if he is asleep. Beside him are the tools of his trade: his helmet, amulet, and bag of dream dust. Throughout the *Sandman* series, Dream is on a quest to reclaim his realm, the Dreaming. This makes him a perfect vehicle for Gaiman to explore myths, cultures, and the human condition.

In *Sandman* number 6, "24 Hours," Doctor Dee uses the amulet to get some unlucky guests at a diner to reveal their innermost secrets and to do horribly violent things to each other. One by one, he kills them off until Dream arrives. Pursuing him into the Dreaming, Doctor Dee throws the amulet at Dream, which destroys it and allows Dream to reabsorb its power. Rendered powerless, Doctor Dee is mercifully returned by Dream to Arkham Asylum.

Sandman number 8 has proven to be one of the most popular *Sandman* stories. Instead of falling back on a traditional image of death as a tall, gloomy male, Gaiman introduces a version who is the short and perky

In *Sandman* number 8, Gaiman introduces Dream's sister Death. This panel shows Dream and Death sitting in a city park, feeding pigeons. Gaiman's depiction of Death is original and daring, showing her to be a smart, spunky, cool older sister who helps guide the troubled Dream through his missions.

older sister to tall, gloomy Dream. In *Sandman* number 8, Death drags him on her rounds, as she collects the souls of the deceased. Despite her heavy and painful duties, Death soldiers on. In watching her, Dream learns a lesson about himself, his sister, and their five siblings: "My sister has a function to perform, even as I do. The Endless [Dream's entire family] have their responsibilities. I have responsibilities." Dream is cheered up, as much as he can be, and returns to rebuilding the Dreaming.

Although Dream neither charms nor laughs at much, "Preludes & Nocturnes" introduces a character of some compassion. Neither hero nor antihero, he does pique interest in this evolving world of dreams.

Art and Production Notes

According to Gaiman, it took him six months to write *Sandman* number 1. Why would it take a talented writer so long to craft a forty-page comic?

When a publisher decides to publish a new comic by little-known writers and artists, the publisher may commit to release only eight issues. If those first issues fail to sell, the comic ends. So, the first issue becomes very important in building an audience for the comic.

At the time, superhero comics were the top-sellers, but Gaiman was not interested in writing superhero stories. So how did Gaiman get an audience that read and purchased superhero comics to follow a dark, brooding character through the world of dreams?

Part of the answer lies in the type of story he told in "Preludes & Nocturnes." Dream begins with nothing, just as the reader knows nothing about him. In *Sandman* number 1, his helm, pouch, and amulet are taken from him; very early in "Preludes & Nocturnes," Gaiman establishes three things that Dream must reacquire. Along the way, the reader gets acquainted with Dream and begins to share in his struggle to reclaim his realm. Despite the unusual nature of the main character, the story of "Preludes & Nocturnes" is actually a classic hero tale that feels familiar to comics readers.

Additionally, Gaiman let Dream interact with existing superheroes from the DC universe. During the writing, Gaiman was unsure of whether this blending of universes would work for his comic. As Gaiman says in his interview for *The Sandman*

Companion, "I was walking a tightrope, really. I wanted the series to look enough like a superhero comic to get people who liked superheroes to read it; and I wanted it to look enough like a horror comic to allow me to write the sort of fantasy stories I was interested in writing."

The series found its unique voice in *Sandman* number 6. On its surface, *Sandman* number 6 pushed the boundaries of what was acceptable in terms of adult comic content. Below the surface, Gaiman explored the stories hidden in each character and showed how people who are ordinary in appearance may have extraordinary depths. It was the first of many *Sandman* issues that developed stories about stories.

By the end of the "Preludes & Nocturnes" story line, *Sandman* had sold more issues than any comic of its type since the 1970s. Gaiman's gambles had paid off. By *Sandman* number 10, Gaiman says in *The Sandman Companion*, "I knew in great detail where I was going and how I was going to get there."

Sandman: "The Doll's House" (Numbers 9–16)

Despite their different locations and characters, a main thread connecting *Sandman* numbers 9 through 16 is the Sandman's efforts to rebuild the Dreaming and the human characters' struggles to break down the walls that stand between them. The African queen Nada, for example, breaks down the wall between herself and love and suffers for it. Rose Walker extracts herself

COLLABORATOR: MIKE DRINGENBERG, PENCILLER

When Sam Kieth, the original penciller for *Sandman*, left the team after *Sandman* number 5, his duties were taken over by Mike Dringenberg.

The final draft of a comics script is passed to the penciller, who draws the comic in pencil form. The penciller's work is later passed to the letterer, inker, and colorist before printing.

Within the sketched panels of each page, the penciller creates the visual magic that gives comics their unique appeal. Working in pencil, the project's first artist lays down all of the line artwork to define the shapes of characters, places, and objects in the story.

Since Dringenberg was the penciller on the early issues of *Sandman*, he designed many of the characters of the series. For *Sandman* number 8, Dringenberg designed the visuals for Death, who was inspired by a girl he knew from Salt Lake City, Utah.

from the tangled world of dreams and rejoins her family. Even the Dream Lord himself manages to break down barriers between himself and Robert Gadling when they become friends.

The Stories

Sandman number 9, "Tales in the Sand," summarizes some important elements about the upcoming story line and the rest of the series. In it, Gaiman tells a story about telling a story. Using this technique on occasion in the *Sandman* series, Gaiman reminds the reader that all stories are beholden to the traditions of oral history, mankind's first means of explaining his universe.

For many readers, the most alarming story in the entire *Sandman* series is *Sandman* number 14, "The Collectors," which features a serial killer known as the Corinthian, a terrible creation of Dream. The Corinthian escaped the Dreaming and now consumes the eyeballs of young boys through mouths located where his own eyes should be. At the close of the serial convention at which he is the keynote speaker, the Corinthian is interrupted by the arrival of Dream, who walks in and "uncreates" him. The final image of the Corinthian is as a tiny skull pinched between Dream's fingers. As he notes in *The Sandman Companion*, Gaiman had a clear objective in developing the story, "Serial killing had not yet been depicted as hip and groovy, but I could see that coming; for example, I'd begun noticing serial killer fanzines, complete with prison interviews. And I wanted to say, 'This isn't hip, this isn't cool.'"

Art and Production Notes

A significant challenge for Gaiman and penciller Mike Dringenberg in "The Doll's House" was introducing numerous new *Sandman* characters. Soon after we meet them in "The Doll's House," these characters appear in dreams or are having dreams. How are readers able to follow the story lines and dreams of so many different characters?

The Corinthian is "uncreated" by the Sandman in this series of panels from number 14, "The Collectors." We see the horror of the Corinthian's mouth-eyes, his face drooping downward until it dissolves into dust, except for a tiny skull, which Dream pinches between his fingers. He takes the dream of the serial killers from the "sustained fantasies in which [they] are the maltreated heroes of [their] own stories."

A key storytelling tool in comics is the layout, which focuses on the size, positioning, and sequencing of panels across the page. In "The Doll's House," a change of characters or dream worlds usually occurs at the top of a new page. On the previous page is often a brief note mentioning the new character's name.

The reader comes to understand each character through the unique art style and nature of his or her dreams. For example, the characters of Ken and Barbie seem to be the ideal couple, just like the dolls with the same name. However, Ken's dreams have rough edges and center on money and power, while his girlfriend, Barbie, has elaborate golden-colored fantasies. The images of Ken and Barbie's dreams are very different, and they are horrified to see each other's dreams when they collide in a dream vortex accidentally created by the character Rose Walker. It comes as no surprise, then, that Ken and Barbie break up at the end of the story. Their art styles clash literally, and their union fails.

Sandman: "Dream Country" (Numbers 17–20)

Despite the infrequent appearances of the Sandman in this collection, these four short stories secured Gaiman's sparkling reputation as a storyteller. Each tale is rooted in myth, from ancient Greece and Egypt to the legend of the faeries to a world of cats that has never been known by man. For Gaiman, these ancient mythologies are still alive and of value today. As Death says at the end of "Dream Country," "Mythologies take longer to die than people believe. They linger in a kind of dream country that affects all."

Each story explores the dreams of a central character: how they have been fulfilled, how they failed to come true, and the costs of their pursuit.

The Stories

Sandman number 19, "A Midsummer Night's Dream," recounts the first time, in Gaiman's vision, that Shakespeare's play of the same name was staged before a live audience. In *Sandman* number 13, Gaiman's Shakespeare cut a deal with Dream; in exchange for the gift of writing plays that would last for centuries, Shakespeare agreed to write two plays for Dream. *A Midsummer Night's Dream* is his first.

In this story within a story, Shakespeare's traveling troupe of actors performs before an audience of Faerie creatures, who are depicted as themselves in the play. Dream tells Titania that, through Shakespeare, the Faerie people will not be forgotten, "[t]hat King Auberon and Queen Titania will be remembered by mortals, until this age is gone." As the play is concluding, however, Dream wonders to Queen Titania if he has done the right thing in his bargain with Shakespeare: "But he does not understand the price. Mortals never do. They only see the prize, their heart's desire, their dream . . . But the price of getting what you want, is getting what you once wanted."

In acquiring one's dreams, one loses them, for they are no longer dreams. In pursuing immortality through dreaming up plays, Shakespeare has neglected the life around him, including his son, Hamnet. Gaiman suggests that for this neglect, Shakespeare paid the price. In real life, Hamnet Shakespeare died in 1596 at the age of eleven. *Sandman* number 19, "A Midsummer Night's Dream," earned the 1991 World Fantasy Award for best short story, the first time the award was given to a comic.

Sandman number 20, "Façade," reveals the disfigured Rainie Blackwell, whose life has been transformed by a gift from the sun god Ra. In her original incarnation in the DC universe, Rainie Blackwell became Element Girl, a powerful superhero. Instead of allowing her newfound gifts to improve her life like a standard superhero would, Rainie Blackwell remains stuck on an old image of herself as a beautiful young woman. Since Ra's gift has made her immortal, she turns to Ra, hidden behind the sun, to ask for her release from life. As he does, she remarks, "I never realized it before. The sun. It's just a mask, too. And the face behind it . . . it's beautiful." Only in death does Rainie see the beauty in the gift of the sun god. As Gaiman explains his reason for telling the story in *The Sandman Companion*: "You want to say to [someone like Rainie], 'But you're amazingly cool and powerful. You can do anything. And yet you're living in a one-room flat [apartment], scared to go out.'"

This panel shows Colleen Doran's immortal Rainie Blackwell from "Façade," as she is released from life. Death stands beside a number of masked beings, watching. In subsequent panels, Rainie dissolves to the floor, and only her mask remains intact. Smugly, Death answers Rainie's phone and tells the caller she can't take a message because Rainie has "gone away, I'm afraid."

Art and Production Notes

Gaiman welcomed the opportunity to write *Sandman* stories that were independent of any story line. In his interview for *The Sandman Companion*, Gaiman notes, "Whenever I was working on a long story line, I'd get several ideas for tales I'd love to write—but wasn't able to because I was in the middle of this bloody long story! So when the story arc was completed, I'd tackle the ideas that I'd put on hold."

Like a magazine, a comics series is sustained by its regular monthly readers, and like a magazine, subscriptions and interest run out. For the price of a single *Sandman* comic, buyers can read a complete tale without committing to a longer story line.

Gaiman used short stories as a means of beginning work with new artists. In *Sandman* number 17, "Calliope," and *Sandman* number 20, "Façade," *Sandman* readers are taken into the personal hells of two women. Although Gaiman's dialogue conveys much of their troubles, the pain and hope of Calliope and Rainie Blackwell arrive on the page through the pencils of Kelley Jones and Colleen Doran.

For Kelley Jones, the key to the "Calliope" story was finding the right depiction of the imprisoned muse. This beautiful woman of Greek mythology has been imprisoned and repeatedly raped for decades. The eyes of Calliope—depicted by Jones as haunted, shadowed, or closed in the story—betray the evil wrought by her captor's desire for greatness.

For "Façade," penciller Colleen Doran spent hours working on the character of Rainie Blackwell. As Doran says in her interview for *The Sandman Companion*, "A penciller does more than design a character's look. She has to get inside the character, to figure out the right body language and subtleties of facial expression . . . Those first five pages show a constantly repeating cycle of despair. It's a very unsettling and appropriate opening for a story in which the protagonist ends up killing herself."

Sandman: "Season of Mists" (Numbers 21-28)

The prologue to the fourth *Sandman* story line opens with Destiny walking alone in his garden. There, Gaiman writes, "You make a choice; and every choice determines future paths." When Dream is persuaded to free Nada from hell, he is resigned: "Very well, then. My course is clear." Dream makes his choice, and in so doing, he changes the direction of "Season of Mists."

The Stories

As suggested by the title, mists swirl around the intentions of characters. Why does Desire conspire against Dream? Why does Lucifer abandon hell and give it to Sandman? Large and powerful forces are in motion, and they will not come to rest for several *Sandman* seasons.

Inside the gates of hell, Dream finds an empty realm except for Lucifer who is closing all of hell's gates. When he finishes, Lucifer gives the key to Dream and has Dream saw off his wings. As he fades from hell, Lucifer says, "I could have told you that I hoped it would bring you happiness. But somehow . . . somehow I doubt it will."

An army of gods and other creatures petition, bribe, and threaten Dream for the key to hell. A huge responsibility has been placed on the shoulders of a character for whom responsibility weighs heavily—exactly what vengeful Lucifer intended. Lucifer has given Dream the key to Dream's own personal hell.

In the middle of "Season of Mists" is the story of Charles Rowland, the boy left at the English boarding

COLLABORATOR: DANIEL VOZZO, COLORIST

Starting in chapter 2 of "Season of Mists," Daniel Vozzo joined the *Sandman* production team as colorist and performed that job for nearly all of the remaining issues in the series.

After a comic has been drawn, inked, and lettered, the colorist adds color to the art to give the comic a sense of depth, place, and tone. At the time, Vozzo painted on watercolor reproductions of the pages. These pages were sent to companies that specialize in color separation.

To print a colored image on a traditional printing press, it must be broken down into four layers of color: cyan, magenta, yellow, and black. Overlapping these four layers effectively mixes colors, which can produce more colors than the human eye can distinguish. Using only four different colors of inks, printers can reproduce the lush colored panels of comics at a reasonable price.

Now, comics colorists work almost exclusively on computers, on which programs like Adobe Photoshop can mathematically generate the subtle tones of watercolor and automatically create color separations, which saves money.

Charles Rowland, a character Gaiman based loosely on himself and his experiences in boarding school, is haunted by ghosts outside his dormitory in these panels from "Season of Mists." After he dies, Rowland cheerfully tells a friend, "[W]e might as well make the most of it."

school. Charles Rowland is in hell. As the ghosts of the dead freed from hell return to the school, they begin to torture the living. Hazed by three older boys, Rowland retreats to the attic, where he dies of cold and starvation. Death arrives to escort him away, yet he refuses to go. Free from Death's hold, Rowland persuades Paine, a ghost who has befriended Rowland, to make a choice to release them from the hell that is their school.

As Rowland and Paine climb out of the attic and leave the school, the ghosts of the older boys begin to torment the weakest among them. As Rowland notes: "They're doing the same things they always did. They're doing it to themselves. That's Hell." While a principal theme of "The Doll's House" was an exploration of the walls between people, Gaiman suggests in "Season of Mists" that walls can be constructed within the individual to keep one entrapped in a prison of one's own making.

The final three stories resolve Dream's great problem of what to do with the key to hell. In the end, Dream is relieved of his responsibility by two angels, who are sent by the Creator to replace Lucifer in hell. However, relief is not without costs; Dream pays for his actions in story lines for several years to come.

Art and Production Notes

In "Season of Mists," Gaiman introduces a host of new characters from a variety of mythologies. In comics, you obviously cannot hear a character's speaking voice. How do comics artists put sound on a page? The answer is in the color and shape of the letters and word balloons for each character, designed by the comic's letterer. No one in comics is better at this key function than Todd Klein.

Letters in a consistent style and size are collectively called a font. For the *Sandman* series, Klein designed fifty different fonts, including the white-on-black style of Dream's speech. In comics, fonts lend a great deal to the expression of character. For example, in chapter 3 of "Season of Mists," the characters of Order and Chaos are presented next to each other on the same page. The background artwork is simple, yet the reader can clearly see the differences between the characters in the fonts used to describe their thoughts.

Additionally, Order and Chaos have different types of word balloons. Word balloons for Order are neat rectangles that form a clean line down the length of the page. On the other side of the page, Chaos's thoughts are contained in jagged forms that seem to pop up all over the panel. The background behind them changes and flows through the word balloons on the page.

In Klein's estimation, at least 75 percent of lettering in comics is now done on the computer. Still, according to Klein, learning to letter by hand is the best way to develop the skills.

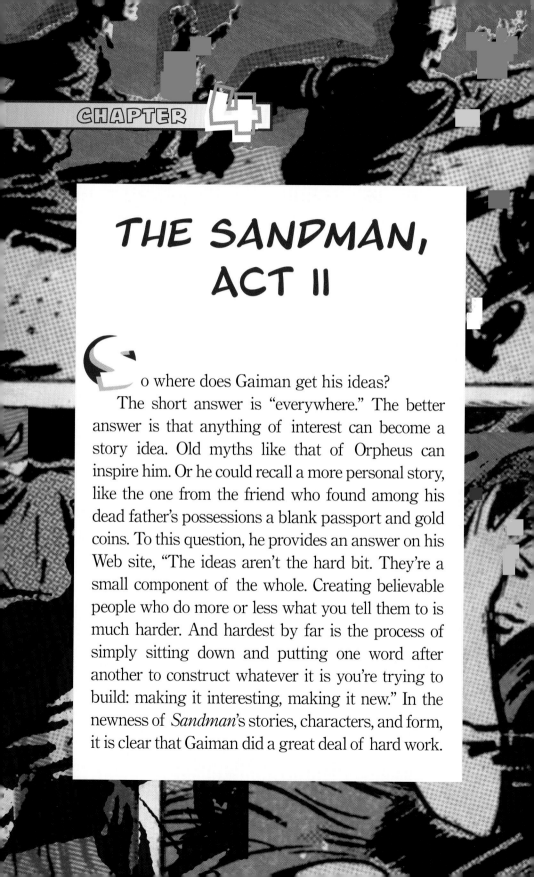

CHAPTER 4

THE SANDMAN, ACT II

So where does Gaiman get his ideas?

The short answer is "everywhere." The better answer is that anything of interest can become a story idea. Old myths like that of Orpheus can inspire him. Or he could recall a more personal story, like the one from the friend who found among his dead father's possessions a blank passport and gold coins. To this question, he provides an answer on his Web site, "The ideas aren't the hard bit. They're a small component of the whole. Creating believable people who do more or less what you tell them to is much harder. And hardest by far is the process of simply sitting down and putting one word after another to construct whatever it is you're trying to build: making it interesting, making it new." In the newness of *Sandman*'s stories, characters, and form, it is clear that Gaiman did a great deal of hard work.

Sandman: "A Game of You" (Numbers 32-37)

Within the first nine pages of "A Game of You," Gaiman introduces ten new characters. Over the course of the collection, Gaiman explores the identities of these characters: how they see themselves, what they show of themselves to the world, and how they live in their own dreams. "A Game of You" is about how these pieces of identity—one's mental, physical, and dream identities—interact on a chessboard of reality and fantasy.

The Stories

Waking from a dreamless sleep on page one is Barbie, last seen in "The Doll's House." At the end of that story line, Barbie's dream world is revealed to be anything but plastic. That dream world comes to life in "A Game of You." As Gaiman says in *The Sandman Companion*, "A lot of the fun of Barbie was taking this person who's such a cliché and then showing that she really isn't; that even someone so apparently shallow has incredibly rich worlds inside of her."

Moving into a rundown apartment building in New York City, Barbie discovers her neighbors are not as they seem to be. So repeats one of Gaiman's themes: inside ordinary people can be extraordinary things, both good and bad.

Each character in the rooming house hides a secret identity. For example, Wanda was born Alvin, a man. Foxglove used to be Donna, and her girlfriend, Hazel, is pregnant. The bookish Thessaly is a centuries-old witch of great power. Central to the struggles of these female characters, is the issue of their names.

For Wanda, the name she creates for herself is the difference between being a man and a woman, between feelings of imprisonment and happiness. At the conclusion of the story, Barbie crosses out "Alvin" on the tombstone and replaces it with "Wanda" in bright pink lipstick. Both her journey to Kansas and Alvin's journey to acceptance as Wanda are complete. Empowered by her dead friend, Barbie seeks a new life and identity of her own.

Thessaly, on the other hand, refuses to reveal or acknowledge her real name, which can be used against her by other witches. All of these characters have found safety and comfort in their new identities and strength in choosing their own names. For each of them, their notions of reality are defined by themselves and are often deeply connected to interior fantasy worlds. Yet those fantasy worlds must change, too. Barbie's childhood dream world dies at the end of the story, an even that is necessary for her to finally arrive in adulthood.

For many readers, "A Game of You" is their least favorite *Sandman* story line. The story's creator, however, enjoyed it. As Gaiman notes in *The Sandman Companion*, "I love the way that it's funny and sad at the same time. I guess the main reason it may be my favorite, though, is that I had this thing in my head that I wanted to do, and at the end I'd done it . . . 'A Game of You' turned out to be almost precisely what I'd hoped for."

This dramatic panel from "A Game of You" is an example of magic realism. A cartoon monster, Martin Tenbones, is placed in a very realistic setting of New York City. The havoc Tenbones wreaks on an immediately recognizable city sidewalk setting is somehow chilling, and the cinematic quality of this panel could easily stand in for a still from a monster movie.

Art and Production Notes

This collection of stories shares some characteristics with a movement in art and literature called magic realism. In art, magic realism covers several types of painting in which objects are reproduced in a natural style, yet they are placed next to elements of fantasy or arranged in unrealistic ways. Gaiman's gold creature Martin Tenbones crashing into the realistic New York City is an image in this tradition.

These stories are not strictly from magic realism, as Gaiman weaves elements from mainstream fiction, fantasy, and horror. To bring his sophisticated story line to life, Gaiman chose artist Shawn McManus. McManus had drawn *Swamp Thing* number 32, one of Gaiman's favorite comics. *In The Sandman Companion*, Gaiman remembers this comic as one that "demanded an artist who could draw both cute fantasy and realistic horror, and mix them seamlessly." This quality was exactly what Gaiman needed for "A Game of You."

Gaiman and McManus nail the horror elements in the story line. Like many readers, the women watching Thessaly's witchcraft are revolted. When Hazel asks Thessaly if it's New Age stuff, the witch replies, "New Age? No. Quite the opposite, really." In *The Sandman Companion*, Gaiman explains this ancient witch: "I'd noticed a movement in some neopagan circles to reinterpret historical witchcraft, making it into some completely bloodless, sweet religion about female empowerment . . . I thought it would be interesting to show one of those women in contemporary times, and have her still behave in a bloody and lethal manner. And not by flying around on a broomstick with a black cat, either, but by following a Greek code of values going back 3,000 years."

What the modern reader may assume about witchcraft is turned upside down by the gruesome rites dating from 3,000 years ago that Thessaly performs. Through horror's ability to grab the reader's attention, Gaiman shows how the ugly or unpleasant bits of mythologies can get sweetened or dropped altogether over time. While he constantly reinterprets old stories and mythologies, Gaiman suggests here that if reinterpretation is done carelessly, truths can be lost.

Sandman: "Fables and Reflections" (Numbers 29–31, Numbers 38–40, Number 50)

In "Fables and Reflections," Gaiman has assembled a collection of tales about human endeavor, its relationship to the world of dreams, and the tales told of it. Occurring out of sequence in the *Sandman* series, these short stories revolve around quests by individuals in leadership positions. The main characters of these stories struggle with questions about choice, how dreams do and do not provide answers, and the consequences of success or failure in their choices.

The Stories

Originally bundled together as "Distant Mirrors," four stories found in the "Fables and Reflections" collection explore how the dreams of leaders affect decisions facing them. Gaiman asks his readers to look in these distant mirrors for lessons for the modern world.

In *Sandman* number 50, "Ramadan," Haroun, the caliph of Baghdad, summons Dream because he wishes to preserve his magnificent city forever. To immortalize his city, Dream tells him: "All you need to do is tell your people. They follow you, after all. And yours is the dream." Haroun makes his proclamation to the people, and when he wakes the next day, the

The caliph of Baghdad takes the Sandman on a magic carpet tour of his city in this beautiful panel from "Ramadan," drawn by P. Craig Russell. "It is a city of marvels, of wonders," the caliph says in the following panel. "I am responsible for it." His desire to immortalize his city leads to its destruction, and the artwork showing the new Baghdad strongly contrasts the magical, vibrant drawing shown here.

Baghdad around him is dark and shabby. Haroun discovers Dream holding the Baghdad of a day before in a glass bottle. Enchanted, he leaves Dream and the bottle utterly happy without knowing why. The story cuts to a modern version of bombed-out Baghdad, in which a young boy hears the final words of the story. Like the caliph of the story, he too leaves utterly happy. Even though his environment is in ruins, he is kept content by the dreams in stories.

One of the tasks of leadership, Gaiman suggests, is to provide a dream or a vision for the people to follow.

COLLABORATOR: P. CRAIG RUSSELL, ARTIST

Considered the favorite *Sandman* story by many fans, *Sandman* number 50, "Ramadan," delivers a magical tale of the caliph of Baghdad. It sold more than 250,000 copies, thanks in part to the pencils and pens of artist P. Craig Russell.

To get the rhythm and feel of the tale of the *Arabian Nights*, Gaiman began developing the project first as a prose short story. When Gaiman read the partial short story to him over the phone, Russell suggested that Gaiman hand him the completed short story as the final script.

Having adapted Rudyard Kipling's *Jungle Book* to comics, Russell knew how to break down a prose story into comic form. He created his own layouts for each page and added colorful touches that Gaiman had not imagined.

While the caliph's dream of immortality for ancient Baghdad does come true, his dream, passed on to the boy in modern Baghdad, provides something simpler yet more important—it provides hope. In both forms, the dream is equally nourishing, as both the caliph and the boy are filled with happiness while stuck in a ruined city. Although Gaiman did not set out to write a story about the troubles in modern Iraq, *Sandman* number 50 proved to be one of the most popular issues of the series.

Bundled together under the title "Convergence," three tales in this collection explore mysteries as expressed through oral stories from different cultures. For example, in *Sandman* number 38, "The Hunt," Vassily tells his bored American granddaughter a tale from "the old country" of a boy who gave up his dream of the princess and married a woman of "our people." At the end of the story, it's revealed that the boy is Vassily himself. The granddaughter and the modern reader are invited to reconsider the whole story. In *Sandman* number 40, "The Parliament of Rooks," the baby Daniel dreams of a journey to the Dreaming. There, Eve, Cain, and Abel tell him stories, each done in a different art style, of their biblical origins. When Abel reveals to Daniel the mystery behind Cain's story about the parliament of rooks, Cain is angered at the betrayal: "I keep telling you: it's the mystery that endures. Not the explanation."

Taken together, these stories show the power of mystery in tales from the past. In Vassily's story, how the mystery is revealed creates a whole new mystery surrounding him for his granddaughter, thereby giving the story modern life. The revelation of the mystery of Cain's story, however, kills it by turning the magic of the unknown past into plain, dull fact. In mystery, there is above all a sense of hope, of possibility. The way in which the sense of mystery is handled is just as important as what is revealed.

The story of Orpheus was bundled into *Sandman Special*, a forty-eight-page comic released between *Sandman* number 31 and number 32. This retelling of the myth of Orpheus paints Dream as an inflexible and uncaring father, making Orpheus's story even more tragic.

Sandman: "Brief Lives" (Numbers 41-49)

As suggested by the title, the "Brief Lives" story line is the beginning of the end of *Sandman*. The stories contained in this collection explore the notion of change and how it is needed in life. From a London doorway, Dream's sister Del (short for Delirium) rises because, as she says, "I need a change." She begins a quest to find Destruction, her long-lost brother. Dream, who is mourning the loss of his lover, chooses to join his sister's quest for their brother as a distraction. It ends up costing him dearly.

The Stories

The collection begins with Dream's son, Orpheus, whose severed yet immortal head has been kept under guard on the island of Lesbos. The first image of Orpheus's whitened head shows the head on a table next to an ancient vase; both of them are relics of the past. Though life around him continues to change, his life has not changed for 3,000 years. He yearns to die.

In the following pages, Delirium journeys to the realms of Desire and Despair, who refuse to join her in searching for Destruction. Change, they say, does not happen to the Endless. Despair, though, knows that it is a false statement, as she blinds herself so that she doesn't have to see change.

Delirium stands in her London doorway, looking for change. The character is another of Dream's siblings, another member of the Endless. It is Delirium's instability that allows her the one thing that Dream resists and that turns out to be his flaw: change.

Delirium next ventures to the realm of Dream. Change is being forced upon her brother, whose lover has left him. Her feelings for him changed, he said, "It was there in her eyes." Yet he cannot control those feelings and plunges the Dreaming into three weeks of rain to match his mood.

In Dream's realm, Del recalls the moment when she changed from Delight to Delirium, "She was no longer Delight; and the blossoms had already begun to fall in her domain, becoming smudged and formless colors . . . and [Destruction] said, 'Del, it's okay.' And then he shut up, and then she starting giggling uncontrollably . . . Then he

COLLABORATOR: JILL THOMPSON, PENCILLER

*D*on't tell Jill Thompson that comics aren't for girls.

In an interview with Adam Gallardo for the Dark Horse Comics Web site, Thompson recalls her early experiences in the industry: "I remember going to comic conventions when I was about thirteen or fourteen and never seeing another girl my age there. I didn't really think about it. The way I saw it was I was in a room with a bunch of people who had things in common with me."

At the San Diego Comics Convention, Neil Gaiman saw one of her drawings of Death. A year later, Thompson's work appeared for the first time in *Sandman* number 40. She continued penciling for *Sandman* through the "Brief Lives" story line. As Gaiman says in *The Sandman Companion*, "Jill was a terrific match for 'Brief Lives,' and I think she did some of her very best work on it."

In the Dark Horse interview, Thompson recalls her early experiences: "When I heard 'no' while submitting a portfolio, it was always for a reason. My figure drawing wasn't up to par or I needed to work on perspective . . . something technical. I can't ever recall being told I wasn't right for a job because I was a woman."

said, 'Del, things are changing.' She knew it was true. And there was nothing she could do about it."

Destruction, the product of change, carried her through the destruction of her old identity (Delight) and into the creation of her new one (Delirium).

Off go the inflexible Dream and the unstable Delirium in search of Destruction. Along the way, people seem to die around the Endless. In a story in the middle of the story line, even Ishtar, the Egyptian goddess of love, chooses to end her life. When Dream and Delirium arrive, Ishtar is reminded that it has been 2,000 years since her lover, Destruction, left her and, still feeling the pain of that loss, she destroys herself. After 2,000 years of trying to hide from her unwavering feelings, Ishtar chooses not to "just keep going" anymore. The story of Ishtar follows the structure of many *Sandman* graphic novels, in which a story in the middle holds all of the main themes of the entire story line.

Against his own judgment, Dream is directed by Destiny to his son, Orpheus. In exchange for a favor, Orpheus tells his father where to find Destruction. At Destruction's new home, Dream asks why he left his responsibilities. Destruction tells him that preventing change is impossible and is no one's responsibility. For Dream, responsibility is everything, and Destruction's views are confusing. To explain further, Destruction takes them outside and points to the stars, "I like the stars. It's the illusion of permanence, I think. I mean, they're always flaring up and caving in and going out.

But from here, I can pretend . . . I can pretend that things last. I can pretend that lives last longer than moments. Gods come, and gods go. Mortals flicker and flash and fade. Worlds don't last; and stars and galaxies are transient, fleeting things that twinkle like fireflies and vanish into cold and dust. But I can pretend."

In this beautiful two-page spread, Destruction is suggesting that change is inevitable, even for the Endless. While Delirium seems to get it, Dream asks him again why he left, failing to understand anything that Destruction has said.

After Destruction leaves, Barnabas the dog tells Delirium to "cheer up. You know? I mean, life's too short." And that is sufficient for her. Dream, however, returns to his sense of responsibility, to the favor he now owes Orpheus: "I have to kill my son."

And so he does. After Dream ends the life of Orpheus, he is shown with blood running down his arms and hands, turning to red petals on the ground. For, as Despair later says, "You cannot seek Destruction and return unscathed." Dream retires to his private chambers. He tells Lucien: "Tomorrow, I shall work. But not today." Though scarred by the experience, he has not changed his sense of duty.

In a pool of water, Dream washes his bloody hands and sees a vision of his son's last day alive. In seeing terrible tragedy in the bloody pool of water, Dream is overcome by grief. He has killed his own son, in part because of his unwillingness to change. In the mythic landscape of the Endless, there will be consequences.

Founding of Vertigo

When Gaiman's *Sandman* series was launched in 1989, it was clear that it did not fit among comics for kids. Although DC Comics was delighted with the sales figures for *Sandman*, the comic violated accepted standards for comics content in the industry.

In 1954, Dr. Fredric Wertham, a psychiatrist, wrote a book called *Seduction of the Innocent*. In it, he argued that comics were a dangerous influence on young people. At one point, he claimed, "Hitler was a beginner compared to the comic-book industry."

In response to these overstated accusations, comics publishers created a set of standards to police themselves. Comics that followed the Comics Code Authority (CCA) received a special stamp on the cover, which was intended to guide parents toward titles that were free of sexual, violent, and otherwise objectionable content. What was objectionable then seems very tame now. For example, the CCA guidelines included statements like this one: "In every instance good shall triumph over evil and the criminal punished for his misdeeds."

With the success of *Sandman*, however, DC Comics struck a nerve with older audiences ready and able to handle such material. In 1993, DC formed a new imprint, Vertigo Comics, aimed at the mature, literate reader. Edited by Karen Berger, many of these titles were written and drawn by talent Berger found in Britain, artists such as Neil Gaiman and Dave McKean.

Sandman number 48 was the first comic published under the Vertigo name. Revealed at the beginning of the story is the new life of Destruction, the Endless sibling who had rejected the old traditions of the family to become an artist. Although his art is unpolished, Destruction is energized by the freedom to create, just as Gaiman and other comics artists were liberated by Vertigo from the Comics Code Authority.

CHAPTER 5

THE END OF THE SANDMAN'S DREAM

Nine years of breathing life into the characters of *Sandman* month after month had taken a toll on Gaiman. As he notes in *The Sandman Companion*, "There were periods near the end of the series where *Sandman* seemed larger, deeper, more important than my whole life was . . . I remembered all of it, at all times—panel for panel, line for line, word for word . . . It was an enormous relief when the series was completed, because that allowed me to 'unload it from memory.'"

Early in the series, Gaiman estimates that it took about two weeks to complete each script. By the end in 1995, he was struggling to finish a fresh, new script for a single issue in seven weeks. He had done what he had wanted to do in *Sandman*. There was only one place left to take it: the end of Dream.

Rather than compromise the quality of *Sandman*, Vertigo chose to stop publishing the comic when Gaiman left. For a series about the nature of stories, it makes sense that, like all stories, it had to come to an end.

Sandman: "Worlds' End" (Numbers 51-56)

In the eighth collection in the *Sandman* series, "Worlds' End," Gaiman returns to the short story form with a series of tales told by visitors to an inn between worlds. Both the title of the collection and the name of the inn, Worlds' End refers to the shared ending of multiple worlds. Caught in a "reality storm," these human, fairy, and centaur characters share food, drink, and tales at a table in the tavern known as Worlds' End.

The Stories

Each story revolves around a group of people and how these people interact through story. Some of the stories are spells cast over the assembled group. Some of them have meaningful instruction in them. And some are told simply for the pleasure of telling a story. All of them have some ability to change the lives of the listeners.

Of particular interest is "Hob's Leviathan," *Sandman* number 53. "Call me Jim," begins the narration of a sailor on the *Sea Witch* who meets Robert "Hob" Gadling, made immortal by Death several hundred years ago (*Sandman* number 13). On the deck of the ship, Hob tells Jim, "Like the sea, you've got hidden

The New York Times best-selling author of **American Gods** and **Coraline**

NEIL GAIMAN

Volume Eight

THE SANDMAN WORLDS' END

Illustrated by
Michael Allred
Gary Amaro
Mark Buckingham
Dick Giordano
Tony Harris
Steve Leialoha
Vince Locke
Shea Anton Pensa
Alec Stevens
Bryan Talbot
John Watkiss
Michael Zulli

Introduction by
Stephen King

Twelve illustrators worked with Gaiman on *Sandman* numbers 51 through 56 "Worlds' End." With so many *Sandman* collaborators, each having his or her own work style, it was important that Gaiman be organized and flexible. The variety in art styles throughout the series helped bring out the many moods and character shifts in Gaiman's masterwork.

depths. Do you ever wonder about what goes on under there? There's more sea than there is land, after all. And we never see more than the tiniest fraction of it. There's a storm coming."

And he's right. A storm does batter the ship that night, and in the morning, a sea serpent rises from the depths, chasing schools of fish. When Jim says to Hob that they should tell the world the story of the sea serpent, the man who is hundreds of years old tells Jim: "There's tales of sea serpents, after all. But the sea's a big place, Jim, and deep . . . Lots of secrets down there."

Later, on the dock at Aden, Hob reveals that he knows his secret: "Jim" is actually a girl. When Margaret, who has been masquerading as Jim, asks how he knew, Hob says, "a lot of it's learning to see what you see and not what you think you see, if that makes any sense." As an act of friendship, Hob reveals to Margaret that he has lived many lives. When Margaret asks his age, Hob says, "Old enough to have learned to keep my mouth shut about seeing a bloody great snake in the middle of the ocean." Secrets, it seems, are a part of the wonderful mystery of life for Hob Gadling, but that does not mean that he needs to share them with the world.

Within these stories, there are other stories, as well. There is the story of the inn itself, which is constantly changing shape. The innkeeper says: "When a world ends, there's always something left over. A story, perhaps, or a vision, or a hope. This inn is a refuge after the lights go out. For a while."

Art and Production Notes

Like the structure of the stories, the art of the collection is framed around the scenes at "Worlds' End," which were penciled by Bryan Talbot. Talbot's style is fairly representational. He attempts to create realistic characters and locations. Talbot's art is the visual base from which the stories start and to which they return.

This representational base provides a sense of visual stability to this collection. The inn is between worlds, yet the stories told there occur in places and times that are very different from that of the inn. Naturally, the art style of each story changes to reflect its location.

The penciling and inking for the parts outside of the inn were done by different artists on each story. Their styles range from the nervous, dreamlike quality in *Sandman* number 51, "A Tale of Two Cities," to a style more fitting for the era in which "Hob's Leviathan" is set. While it is generally representational, the art style of *Sandman* number 54, "The Golden Boy," is slightly cartoonlike, as the America in his alternate universe is somewhat bizarre when compared to the America in our world. It is a worthwhile exercise to compare the art styles in this collection to see how an artist's style matches the type of story that Gaiman is telling.

Sandman: "The Kindly Ones" (Numbers 57–69)

In "The Kindly Ones," all of Dream's mistakes in earlier stories explode in his face. The Kindly Ones merely come to the Dreaming to witness the self-destruction of Dream.

At thirteen issues in length, the story line of "The Kindly Ones" extended for more than a year in monthly comics. When he was scripting the story, Gaiman knew that it would eventually be bound into graphic novel form. As he remembers in *The Sandman Companion*, "I therefore chose to pace the story in a way that would work perfectly for a book—but that would not work very well for a monthly comic, as it would be too slow at the start and too fast at the end . . . This made it tough even for readers who never missed an issue, because you can forget a lot of plot development in a month, or forget the identity of a character introduced three months ago."

With the knowledge that "The Kindly Ones" would become a bound volume, Gaiman took the rare opportunity to write a rich story that weaves many of the series' characters and subplots into the epic ending of Dream.

For all of the mysterious forces and powerful beings at work in the *Sandman* series, Dream does create his own fate, knowing all along that he is doing it. As far back as *Sandman* number 12, Dream began setting the stage for the transition to a new version of Dream. "One day I will come for it," he tells Lyta Hall about her baby, Daniel. As Death tells Dream in their final meeting: "You have been making [the necessary preparations] for ages. You just didn't let yourself know that was what you were doing."

And then Dream is dead. Like the death of Orpheus, the fall of Dream can be interpreted as a

Instead of the mystical figures of the Fates we are used to seeing in other tragic works, artist Marc Hempel has drawn the Kindly Ones in a more cartoonish and humorous style. They are three distinct but regular-looking women who help Dream play out his story to its logical conclusion. These two panels show the Kindly Ones cutting the Sandman's life thread.

tragedy. Originating in ancient Greece, the dramatic form of tragedy involves a heroic and powerful character who is brought down by a tragic flaw, a weakness in his personality that is exploited by others. In Greek classics, the tragic hero makes choices that seal his fate. The battle between the hero's choices and his fate is often shown as a war between the hero and characters called the Fates. Like these three Greek goddesses of destiny, the Kindly Ones bring down Gaiman's Dream.

One of the magical elements of a well-crafted tragedy is the sense of mystery leading up to its climax. However, as soon as the climax is reached in a fine story such as

Sandman, the reader should immediately feel that, given the choices made by the main character before it, the climax is the only possible outcome for the story. As the characters and universe around him change, Dream's refusal to change, his tragic flaw, places more and more pressure on the Dream King. By the end of the story, it is apparent that Dream should not have been so inflexible in dealing with Lyta Hall in *Sandman* number 12, for she later called the Kindly Ones on him. He should not have accepted the responsibility for the key to hell from Lucifer, since that led to a bargain with the troublesome Loki in *Sandman* number 28. And he should not have been inflexible in the treatment of his son, Orpheus, because when he closed Orpheus's eyes in *Sandman* number 49, he gave the Kindly Ones a reason to end his life. In the end, these pressures overwhelm him, leaving the reader with the feeling that, although the death of this likable character is sad, it does make sense.

Art and Production Notes

Some longtime fans of *Sandman* found the style of penciller Marc Hempel to be unsettling. His blocky shapes and the coloring done by Danny Vozzo were a departure from the art styles that appeared in earlier *Sandman* collections. It was a bold, new take on *Sandman.*

Instead of drawing a realistic and detailed image of a human being, for example, Hempel seeks to represent a face, its expression, and the mood of a panel in the fewest pen strokes possible. Artists like Hempel feel that readers who are captivated by the artwork may be drawn away from the story itself. As Hempel notes in *The Sandman Companion*, "I try to keep the compositions and forms as simple as possible, because I believe everything that appears on the page should service the storytelling."

Gaiman and others were pleased with his results. As P. Craig Russell, artist for the highly decorated *Sandman* number 50, notes in an interview for *The Sandman Companion*, "Marc Hempel is vastly superior to the sort of artist the fans typically idolize. His ability to nail a character in just two or three lines—the expression, the gesture, the mood—is amazing. Fans think that if you draw every leaf on a tree, you're god . . . But what really impresses me is being able to suggest every leaf on a tree with a single line."

Gaiman was pleased as well, saying in *The Sandman Companion*, "There are things Marc and I pulled off that I'm astonishingly proud of."

Sandman: "The Wake" (Numbers 70–75)

"The Wake" brings to an end Gaiman's nine-year exploration of stories, myths, and the world of dreams. The sixty-nine issues that preceded "The Wake" boil down to this slender collection, which honors the passing of one Dream and the rise of the new one who was once Lyta Hall's baby, Daniel. In passing the torch from one version (one "aspect," in the language of the series) of Dream to the next, Gaiman suggests that dreams never really die, and in the gentler, more flexible version of Dream, there remains hope for change in them.

Daniel speaks to the raven, Matthew, in this panel from *Sandman* number 70, "The Wake." Somber and unsure of his new position, he mourns the old Dream. The realm of this new Dream is reflected in an art style that is distinctive from any used in previous *Sandman* installments.

The Stories

In the English language, there are many definitions of the word "wake," and Gaiman uses several of them in the titles of the first three chapters of this collection.

The first story, *Sandman* number 70, "Which occurs in the Wake of What Has Gone Before," describes the wake that trails after Dream's death at the end of "The Kindly Ones." The Endless gather to prepare the funeral for Dream. As many *Sandman* characters fall into dreams to journey to the Dreaming for the funeral, Daniel quickly demonstrates that his reign in the Dreaming will be different from the previous. He gives in to Cain's request to return Abel to life, and he allows Fiddler's Green to remain dead. Unlike the previous Dream, he shows flexibility by giving choices to others.

In the second story, *Sandman* number 71, "In Which a Wake Is Held," Dream's family and friends gather for a wake. In this traditional ceremony, they speak about Dream the night before the funeral. Matthew, Dream's raven, avoids the wake, refusing to acknowledge that Dream is gone. When Matthew asks Lucien why Dream had to die, Lucien says, "Sometimes, perhaps, one must change or die. And in the end, there were, perhaps, limits to how much he could let himself change." In these words, Lucien has captured the tale of Dream.

In the third chapter, *Sandman* number 72, "In Which We Wake," the funeral for Dream is completed, and the people who attend it wake up from their dreams into a new beginning. As the ceremony begins, Destruction visits Daniel to offer his advice, "It's astonishing how much trouble one can get oneself into, if one works at it. And astonishing how much trouble one can get oneself out of, if one simply assumes that everything will, somehow or other, work out for the best."

In the Dreaming, the new Dream admits Lyta Hall to his chambers. Dream forgives Lyta, whose actions cost the new Dream his mortal life, and promises his protection for the remainder of her life. Matthew arrives and says, "Funeral's over. Time to get on with our lives. Time to grow up." He chooses to stay in the Dreaming. The humans who attended the funeral begin to wake up, and Matthew escorts Dream to his first meeting with the other Endless.

In *Sandman* number 73, "Sunday Morning," Hob Gadling goes with his girlfriend to a Renaissance fair, a modern re-creation of a Renaissance festival. As a 600-year-old man, Hob is disgusted with how inaccurate the modern version is. He complains about all of the flaws to his girlfriend, a black woman. Several hundred years ago, Hob traded slaves from Africa to the New World, yet he has changed to accept a black woman into his life. Although Hob has seen many friends die and feels out of place in modern times, he nevertheless rejects Death's offer to end it all, choosing instead to carry forward with his new love.

In the final story of the collection, *Sandman* number 75, "The Tempest," William Shakespeare is hard at work on finishing the final play of his legendary career and trying to manage life with his wife and daughter. Hurt by his continuous writing and daydreaming, Shakespeare's wife and daughter have given up on Will. In his own life, he has become an island—isolated from his family by his gift to give a voice to dreams. When Dream comes to collect the completed *Tempest* from Shakespeare, the writer asks him why he wanted such a play. Dream says, "I wanted a tale of graceful ends. I wanted a play about a King who drowns his books, and breaks his staff, and leaves his kingdom. About a magician who becomes a man. About a man who turns his back on magic."

When Shakespeare presses him further, Dream replies, "Because I will never leave my island." Like Shakespeare, Dream is caught in the world of dreams— a place inside each of us that can be shared with others only in small amounts, only for as long as we remember them. Through their work, both Shakespeare and Gaiman have given us dreams worthy of memory.

Letting Go

And then it was over. After seventy-six issues (including *Sandman Special*), the story of Sandman came to a close. In an introduction to "The Endless," Gaiman summarizes his landmark series, "The Lord of Dreams learns that one must change or die, and makes his decision."

Dream makes the choice that he does not change, and he pays the ultimate price. At some point during the *Sandman* series, Gaiman the writer must have realized that he faced the same choice. While his mortal life was not in danger, his artistic life was at risk. As he mentions in an interview with the *Talking Volumes* radio program, "I get very bored very quickly at the point where I think I know what I'm doing and the point where I feel like I'm not making any more interesting mistakes and learning from them. The joy for me is to move from medium to medium where I can keep making absolutely different sets of mistakes and learning from them."

As Dream moved on to the next phase of his existence, so, too, did his creator, Neil Gaiman.

Although Gaiman is no longer writing monthly issues of *Sandman*, new stories featuring Dream and other *Sandman* characters have appeared. While Gaiman has written some of them and reviewed others, he has moved into other realms. Indeed, several years before the end of *Sandman*, he had begun, like Dream, to lay out plans for change.

CHAPTER 6

OTHER MYTHS, NEW DREAMS

E ven during the *Sandman* years, Gaiman still managed to develop other comics projects and to write in different forms. In the middle of the *Sandman* years, he made perhaps the biggest change of all.

The Tragical Comedy or Comical Tragedy of Mr. Punch

Released in 1995, *The Tragical Comedy or Comical Tragedy of Mr. Punch* deserves special mention because Gaiman has called it his favorite graphic novel. The title itself gives a clue to the story; is it a comical tragedy or a tragic comedy? The answer, of course, is that it is neither. The truth lies somewhere between the types of story, which is a familiar place for Gaiman readers.

In England, *Punch and Judy* puppet shows have been a mainstay of entertainment for 300 years. Together, the acerbic Punch and his long-suffering wife, Judy, unleashed stories, slapstick humor, and crude jokes on audiences that have loved them for centuries. Gaiman, of course, has a different take on this familiar story.

The Story of Mr. Punch

An adult narrator recounts a story of a summer spent with his grandfather, who ran an arcade in Southsea, England. The haunting landscape of the boardwalk is colored by the desolate state of the arcade; no one is coming to see the featured mermaid or the *Punch and Judy* show. Professor Swatchell, the professor of the *Punch and Judy* show, and his assistant seem to have secret knowledge of affairs at the arcade and of the boy's grandfather. Repeatedly, the boy's elders hide the truth from him. The narrator says, "I lived in a land of giants in those days. All children do. In a perfect world, it occurs to me now, i [sic] would write this book in blood, not ink. One cannot lie, if one writes in blood. There is too much responsibility: and the ghosts of those one has killed will rise up and twist the pen down true lines, change the written word to the unwritten as the red lines fade on the page to brown."

The adult narrator realizes that he cannot recapture the truth of the "giants" of his childhood. In effect, the narrator admits that recollection in true, original form is not possible.

The rest of the story slowly peels back the layers of family history and tragedy that are kept hidden from the young boy. His grandfather and the *Punch and Judy* professor have a shared past, yet it is not until the closing of the arcade that the boy learns of his grandfather's crimes. Peering into an arcade window, the boy sees into the troubled world of his grandfather, whose pregnant girlfriend, the mermaid, is punched by two mysterious men, while his grandfather watches helplessly. When they return to the car, the grandfather tells him, "You didn't see anything." Just as childhood events are hidden by uncertain memory, so, too, are the most traumatic ones hidden by a child's lack of understanding and an adult's desire to protect him or her from it. Indeed, the identities and motives of the other two men remain a permanent mystery to the narrator.

Years later, the narrator happens across a gathering of *Punch and Judy* professors. Through the crowd, he glimpses someone who looks like Professor Swatchell. Then the face is gone. When he asks one of the other professors about Professor Swatchell, the man produces a swatchell, a device used by the puppeteer to produce the voice of Mr. Punch. This adult figure from his childhood, Professor Swatchell, is lost forever. The narrator fails to connect the people in his current world back to the past. Like the audience at a puppet show, the narrator cannot see the whole truth of the story, which is partially hidden in his memory. Or, as Gaiman says in an interview with the *Baltimore Sun* newspaper, "Children are in a world in which much of what's going on is not only unknown but unknowable. People are not explaining things and you lack the information to make sense of things even if they did explain them."

Art and Production Notes

For *Mr. Punch*, artist Dave McKean mixes photography, painting, sketching, and collage to create somewhat haunted images whose tone lingers in memory far after the actual image has faded.

Since the story is experienced through childhood memories, it makes sense that the human figures in the stories would appear in an almost cartoon style. For most people, memories from childhood are patchwork; some things, like traumatic events or favorite toys, linger in memory well into adulthood. The faces of our family, friends, and even ourselves, though, fade into less distinct shapes. These memories are often colored by memories from the present. A few pages into the story, for example, the adult narrator is depicted looking very much like the child.

In contrast to the drawings, the Punch and Judy puppets were photographed by McKean. These pictures were then manipulated for storytelling purposes. In an interview with the *Baltimore Sun* newspaper, McKean suggests his reasoning: "Generally people tend to think that photographs tell the truth, that they're honest, and they're clearly not. There are huge amounts of editing going on all the time with photographs. Because they have this veneer of reality, they are probably all the more insidious. All the dreams and the nightmares and the sort of odd puppet shows I ended up photographing so they have an illusion of reality. It's really just to play with people's expectations."

Mixing different art media gives *The Tragical Comedy or Comical Tragedy of Mr. Punch* a haunting, dreamlike quality that makes the reader unsure of what is real, what is reliable, and what is a false memory.

With the Punch and Judy puppets, McKean is attempting to trigger memories of childhood, for British readers at least. Yet, like the images of the story, those memories are twisted. He notes in the *Baltimore Sun*, "I think it's because you tend to remember your childhood in these tiny little fragments of time and very often you're not even remembering real things anymore." One character might appear in three different forms— painted, drawn, or photographed.

Despite the various forms in play, McKean somehow maintains enough elements of consistency between images of the same character so that readers can follow the flow of the story for each character without difficulty. While the narration of the story is quiet, it is the striking nature of McKean's images that keeps the reader's eyes fixed to the page.

Neil Gaiman took this photograph of artist and frequent collaborator Dave McKean. The effect is menacing and haunting, and brings to mind a wounded animal held prisoner in a cage. This photograph appears in the back of *Black Orchid*.

Moving to the Land of Myth

In 1992, Gaiman and his wife decided to move to Minnesota, so that their children could be closer to her family. In an interview with *January Magazine*, Gaiman notes that the move to America realized one of his dreams: "I thought, you know, if I'm going to leave England and go to America, I want one of those things that only America can provide and one of those things is *Addams Family* houses."

At home, his most productive writing location is a small octagonal structure at the far end of the garden, overlooking the woods. In an interview with Danger Media Guild, Gaiman describes the place: "[It] has nothing in it but a desk, a chair, a heater, a little CD player, and a dictionary . . . It's completely boring, and that's probably the place that I get the most stuff done . . . My only rule is that if I'm there, I can either do nothing, or I can work. So, I can sit there for fifteen minutes and stare out the window, and after that you get bored, so you may as well start writing."

By limiting the outside distractions, Gaiman can focus on the ideas coming from within. In an office in the basement of the house, Gaiman stores his large collection of books, notebooks, CDs, and his computer. Later in the evening, he migrates with his laptop to the television room upstairs.

Broader Horizons: Novels

While Gaiman's first success came in comics, he never intended to limit himself to that medium. As early as 1984, he was publishing short stories in British science-fiction magazines, and in 1990, he cowrote *Good Omens* with science-fiction and fantasy writer Terry Pratchett. His 1996 novel *Neverwhere* followed London office worker Richard Mayhew deep below ground on a quest to rescue the Lady Door, a royal figure of the underground. Doors reappear in his 2003 children's story, *Coraline*, when a young girl opens a boarded-up door in her new house to discover a new and dangerous world behind it. Similarly, in *Stardust*, young Tristan Thorn goes behind the wall that towers over his town to chase a star fallen deep in the land of Faerie. In each of these stories, a young person is confronted with a door or other force through which he or she finds a dream world that changes his or her real one.

Each Gaiman novel shows a broadening and deepening of ability in the form. In 2001, Gaiman released

In 2002, Neil Gaiman accepted the Hugo Award for his novel *American Gods*. The Hugo is France's most prestigious honor for science-fiction achievement. *American Gods* also won the Bram Stoker Award for Best Horror Novel, the Locus Award for Best Fantasy Novel, and the Nebula Award, given by the Science Fiction and Fantasy Writers of America.

American Gods, a journey through the mythic and real heartland of America. The first novel that he wrote from scratch by himself, *American Gods* received the 2002 Hugo Award for Best Science-Fiction/Fantasy Novel. In an interview for the Barnes and Noble Web site, Gaiman is characteristically modest about the book, "In many ways right now, writing novels is the next form I'm trying to master. I felt like I got pretty good at comics, and I'm fairly comfortable with my ability to write short stories. *American Gods* is the first novel I've written that I felt I was beginning to show any sign of talent at the medium."

Miracleman and 1602

In 1986, Gaiman received a call from Alan Moore, who no longer wanted to write his *Marvelman* comic and was willing to let Gaiman take it over. Honored to be continuing Moore's comic, Gaiman penned *Marvelman* (known as *Miracleman* in the United States) for three years. Moore assigned to him his one-third share of the rights to the comic.

When *Miracleman* publisher Eclipse Comics went bankrupt, Todd McFarlane, publisher of Image Comics, purchased the Eclipse share of the rights to the comic. In payment for work on other projects, McFarlane offered to Gaiman his rights to the critically acclaimed series. However, they later became embroiled in a fight over those rights. In October 2002, a court decided that those rights belonged to Gaiman. Marvel Comics became involved.

In exchange for Gaiman agreeing to produce eight issues of a new comic called *1602*, Marvel agreed to donate all of its proceeds from the comic to Marvels and Miracles, a company that Gaiman and Marvel CEO Joe Quesada set up to assist in the legal costs of resolving the *Miracleman* rights.

After he agreed to do *1602* to help resolve the dispute, Gaiman began looking for an idea. Then the September 11, 2001, terrorist attacks happened. At the press conference announcing the new title, Gaiman recalled his thinking for the story, "I decided that whatever I did, given the mood I was in at that point, it wasn't going to have sky-scrapers, it wasn't going to have bombs, and it probably wasn't going to have any guns or planes in it . . . As soon as I put that together, the ideas of *1602* sort of fell straight into my head."

Set in England in 1602, the series features historical figures from the era, as well as versions of familiar Marvel superheroes as they might have existed in the seventeenth century. Readers familiar with the X-Men, Beast, and Iceman will find their equivalents in *1602*.

Films

A number of Gaiman's stories have been in Hollywood hands for years. Finally, some of them are reaching the big screen. After a particularly bad experience in Hollywood, Gaiman and coauthor Terry Pratchett did not issue options on their novel *Good Omens* for several years. When Terry Gilliam, the creator of *Brazil* among other films, became involved, Gaiman and Pratchett promptly turned over control of the project to Gilliam entirely. Gaiman claims that he and Pratchett want nothing to do with the project at all: "It's Terry Gilliam. I'm very happy to see whatever he does."

The British Broadcasting Company produced a miniseries in 1996 for *Neverwhere*, Gaiman's novel of life under London. With Dave McKean, Gaiman wrote *MirrorMask*, a story about a fifteen-year-old girl in a family circus, and McKean has directed the film.

Gaiman was given the job of adapting the script of *Princess Mononoke*, a Japanese animated feature about a young girl who has been raised by wolves, for English-speaking audiences. The movie's clever story line and amazing animation delighted American moviegoers.

Gaiman also wrote the English-language script for *Princess Mononoke*, an animated feature directed by Miyazaki Hayao. Released in the United States in 1997, *Princess Mononoke* has received wide acclaim for its gorgeous animation and Gaiman's careful scripting.

It is not surprising that a satisfactory script for a *Sandman* film has yet to emerge. Several teams have taken options on *Sandman*, but, as Gaiman says in *The Sandman Companion*, "To make it film-shaped, it's like taking a baby and cutting off both of its arms and one of its legs and nose and trying to cram it into this little box, and filling the rest of the box up with meat. I don't think it works that way."

Comic Book Legal Defense Fund

Founded in 1986 by publisher Denis Kitchen, the Comic Book Legal Defense Fund (CBLDF) protects the rights for artists to produce comics and for sellers to sell them. The CBLDF maintains a guiding principle that "comics should be accorded the same constitutional rights as literature, film, or any other form of expression."

Starting in 1993, Gaiman began the Guardian Angel Tour series of readings to support the CBLDF. In 1997, he was named a "defender of liberty" by the CBLDF for his contributions to the protection of individual artists. Gaiman was appointed to the CBLDF Board of Directors in 2000.

The Next Dreams

The boy who hid with a book under the table at family parties has become a small industry of his own. Each project that Gaiman touches seems to draw more fans to his work. Despite such worldwide acclaim, Gaiman has managed to keep his ego in control. In discussing his considerable fame with Danger Media Guild, Gaiman says, "These days, I tend to regard it as a kind of fortune. I write the kind of stories that I would like to read, that nobody's writing. So, I write them with an audience of me in mind. I'm very lucky . . ."

Luck may have played a part in Gaiman's career. Certainly, bringing people such as Dave McKean, Alan Moore, and Karen Berger into his professional life may was a shrewd move. But perhaps Gaiman has achieved such grand success mostly because he responded to the power of his dreams. He heard them, found them, doggedly followed them, and let them change him in the process. Consistently, his dreams have carried him into new territory: new ideas to form into words, new myths to shape into story, and new writing forms to master. While his path undoubtedly has had its share of struggles, Gaiman has become a skilled writer with significant abilities in different forms and styles. Whether he's writing a horror short story or a fantasy novel, Gaiman has stuck to what got him there: the mighty power of the dream.

The End

Black Orchid. New York: DC Comics, 1991.

Mr. Punch. New York: DC Comics/Vertigo, 1995.

Sandman: "Brief Lives." New York: DC Comics/ Vertigo, 1994.

Sandman: "The Doll's House." New York: DC Comics, 1990.

Sandman: "Dream Country." New York: DC Comics, 1991.

Sandman: "Fables and Reflections." New York: DC Comics/Vertigo, 1993.

Sandman: "A Game of You." New York: DC Comics, 1993.

Sandman: "The Kindly Ones." New York: DC Comics/Vertigo, 1996.

Sandman: "Preludes and Nocturnes." New York: DC Comics, 1991.

Sandman: "Season of Mists." New York: DC Comics, 1992.

Sandman: "The Wake." New York: DC Comics/ Vertigo, 1997.

Sandman: "Worlds' End." New York: DC Comics/ Vertigo, 1994.

SELECTED AWARDS

Bram Stoker Award (Horror Writers Association)

Best Illustrated (*The Dream Hunters*, 1999)
Best Novel (*American Gods*, 2002)
Best Work for Younger Readers (*Coraline*, 2003)

Eagle Award

Best Graphic Novel (*Violent Cases*, 1988)
Best Writer of American Comics (1990)

GLAAD Award

Best Comic (*Death: The Time of Your Life*, 1996)

Harvey Award

Best Writer (1990 and 1991)
Best Continuing Series (*Sandman*, 1992)

Hugo Award

Winner, Best Science-Fiction/Fantasy Novel (*American Gods*, 2002)
Winner, Best Novella (Coraline, 2003)

Julia Verlanger Award (France)

Best Fantasy/Science-Fiction Novel, (*Neverwhere*, 1999)

Nebula Award
Best Novel (*American Gods*, 2002)

Will Eisner Comic Industry Award
Best Writer (1991, 1992, 1993, 1994)
Best Continuing Series (Sandman, 1991, 1992, 1993)
Best Graphic Album—Reprint (Sandman, "The Doll's House," 1991)
Best Graphic Album (*Signal to Noise*, 1992)
Best Graphic Album—New (*Signal to Noise*, 1993)

World Fantasy Award
Best Short Story (*Sandman* number 19, "A Midsummer Night's Dream," 1991)

GLOSSARY

antagonist A character who stands opposed to the goals of the main character.

climax The peak of a story.

colorist An artist who applies color to the inked drawings of a comic.

contrast The difference in intensity between the light and dark areas in an image.

dialogue In comics, words spoken by the characters.

editor In comics, the person responsible for reviewing and correcting the work of writers and artists and managing the publication process of the comic.

font A group of letters in a consistent style and size.

inker An artist who retraces finished drawings in ink to make them ready for production.

layout The specific arrangement of panels on a page to best tell the story.

osteopath A nontraditional medical professional who manipulates the skeleton and tissue structures to relieve ailments and pain.

palette The set of colors that an artist chooses to use in a work.

penciller The artist who draws the art of each panel in pencil.

protagonist The main character of a story.

setting The location in which a story is placed.

word balloon A bubble on a comics page that contains the thoughts or speech of a character.

FOR MORE INFORMATION

Comic Book Legal Defense Fund
P.O. Box 693
Northampton, MA 01061
(800) 992-2533
Web site: http://www.cbldf.org

Comic-Con International Convention
P.O. Box 128458
San Diego, CA 92112-8458
(619) 491-2475
Web site: http://www.comic-con.org/

International Comic Festival
P.O. Box 48
Clevedon, Bristol BS21 7LQ
United Kingdom
Web site: http://www.comicfestival.co.uk

Museum of Comic and Cartoon Art
594 Broadway, Suite 401
New York, NY 10012
(212) 254 3511
Web site: http://moccany.org/index.html

World Science Fiction Convention

P.O. Box 426159
Kendall Square Station
Cambridge, MA 02142
Web site: http://www.worldcon.org

Web Sites

Due to the changing nature of Internet links, the
Rosen Publishing Group, Inc., has developed an online
list of Web sites related to the subject of this book.
This site is updated regularly. Please use this link to
access the list:

http://www.rosenlinks.com/lgn/nega

FOR FURTHER READING

Bender, Hy. *The Sandman Companion: A Dreamer's Guide to the Award-Winning Comic Series*. New York: DC Comics, 2000.

McCloud, Scott. *Reinventing Comics: How Imagination and Technology Are Revolutionizing an Art Form*. New York: HarperCollins Perennial, 2000.

McCloud, Scott. *Understanding Comics*. New York: HarperCollins, 1993.

Wiater, Stanley, and Stephen R. Bissette. *Comic Book Rebels: Conversations with the Creators of the New Comics*. New York: Donald I. Fine, 1993.

BIBLIOGRAPHY

"About Vertigo." DC Comics. Retrieved March 9, 2004 (http://www.dccomics.com/about/vertigo.html).

Amado, Alex. "Following His Dream: An Interview with Neil Gaiman." *Spray*, March 11, 1991. Retrieved March 31, 2004 (http://biphome.spray.se/rivieran/interviews/alex.html).

Arnold, Andrew D. "The Graphic Novel Silver Anniversary." *Time*, November 14, 2003. Retrieved March 28, 2004 (http://www.time.com/time/columnist/arnold/article/0,9565,542579,00.html).

"Author Neil Gaiman." *Talking Volumes*, Minnesota Public Radio, January 20, 2004. Retrieved March 10, 2004 (http://news.mpr.org/programs/midmorning/listings/mm20040119.shtml).

Bender, Hy. *The Sandman Companion: A Dreamer's Guide to the Award-Winning Comic Series*. New York: DC Comics, 2000.

Frankel, Richard. "*Now That's Rich 2—Stupid Camera I.*" Silver Bullet Comic Books, February 22, 2003. Retrieved March 9, 2004 (http://www.silverbulletcomicbooks.com/soapbox/104534761258338%2Cprint.htm).

Gallardo, Adam. "Interviews: Jill Thompson." Dark Horse Comics. Retrieved March 5, 2004 (http://www.darkhorse.com/news/interviews.php?id=796).

Gertler, Nat, ed. *Panel One: Comic Book Scripts by Top Writers.* Thousand Oaks, CA: About Comics, 2002.

Grineau, Joel. *Comic Book Conundrum, Issues 12–14,* January 23, 1998. Retrieved March 9, 2004 (http://www.sideroad.com/comics/column12.html).

Kwitney, Alisa. *The Sandman: King of Dreams.* San Francisco: Chronicle Books, 2003.

McCune, Arthur. "Meet the Writers: Neil Gaiman." Barnesandnoble.com. Retrieved March 29, 2004 (http://www.barnesandnoble.com/writers/writerdetails.asp?userid=2VQJQP9WDP&cid=883296#bio).

Naile. "Neil Gaiman." Danger Media Guild. Retrieved March 28, 2004 (http://dangermedia.org/innerview/gaiman.html).

NeilGaiman.com. August 2001. Retrieved January 12, 2004 (http://www.neilgaiman.com).

"Punch & Judy History." The Punch and Judy College of Professors. Retrieved March 29, 2004 (http://www.punchandjudy.org/mainframesethistory.htm).

Richards, Linda. "Neil Gaiman." *January Magazine,* August 2001. Retrieved March 8, 2004 (http://www.januarymagazine.com/profiles/gaiman.html).

Rimmels, Beth Hannan. "'Mr. Punch' Team Has Hit on Something." *Baltimore Sun,* December 3, 1994. Retrieved March 29, 2004 (http://www.holycow.com/dreaming/lore/941203_Baltimore_Sun.htm).

"'The Sandman' Creator Neil Gaiman." *Talk of the Nation*, NPR, September 18, 2003. Retrieved March 9, 2004 (http://www.npr.org/features/feature.php?wfId=1435177).

Weiland, Jonah. "Marvel to Publish New Project by Neil Gaiman." Comic Book Resources, October 24, 2001. Retrieved March 29, 2004 (http://www.comicbookresources.com/news/newsitem.cgi?id=566).

Weiland, Jonah. "Marvel's '1602' Press Conference." Comic Book Resources, June 27, 2003. Retrieved March 29, 2004 (http://www.comicbookresources.com/news/newsitem.cgi?id=2406).

Wiater, Stanley, and Stephen R. Bissette. *Comic Book Rebels: Conversations with the Creators of the New Comics.* New York: Donald I. Fine, 1993.

INDEX

About the Author

Steven P. Olson is a freelance writer who lives in Oakland, California. Visit him at http://www.stevenolson.com.

Credits

Designer: Les Kanturek